THE PENN COUNTRY
AND THE CHILTERNS

WEST WYCOMBE.

The
Penn Country and
the Chilterns

By

RALPH M. ROBINSON

Illustrated by

CHARLES J. BATHURST

LONDON: JOHN LANE THE BODLEY HEAD LTD
NEW YORK: DODD, MEAD AND COMPANY

First Published in 1929

Made and Printed in Great Britain by
Hazell, Watson & Viney Ltd. London and Aylesbury

CONTENTS

vii

LIST OF ILLUSTRATIONS

THE PENN COUNTRY
AND THE CHILTERNS

CHAPTER I

SANCTUARY

SOME thirty-five miles north-west of London the Chiltern Hills end in an abrupt escarpment. From Dunstable to Wendover its long green wall of short-cropped turf faces the Vale of Aylesbury, but beyond Princes Risborough, where the white chalk crosses carved on the slope gleam across the plain, it bends gradually to the south and looks westward across the Thames to the White Horse Vale beyond. Its greatest elevation never rises much above 850 feet and the general average is nearer 700; but its sheer descent to the flat fields at the bottom gives it an illusion of far greater altitude. The traveller from the Midlands by Aylesbury, Thame or Dorchester cannot fail to note it as a definite range of hills, distinct enough to rank in any geography textbook. If he knows his England, he will recognize many characteristics which it shares with the downlands of Berkshire or of Sussex, but with a difference. While other downs are bald-headed, with only here and there a scrubby tuft of trees, these are capped by a luxuriant growth of beech-woods which only become thin as they draw near Dunstable.

A range of hills has, of necessity, two sides, and nothing could be more different from this than the long Chiltern slope that inclines towards London. The whole fall from the summit to the Vale covers half a mile or less as measured by the map: but on the south-eastern side it takes some fifteen miles to accomplish the same descent to the valley of the Colne. The escarpment is generally straight and bare, and any streams that flow from it gush out from the bottom, at the junction of the chalk and the greensand. But, once over the top, the thickly wooded

1

slope is scored by numberless watercourses, now bereft of water, which have carved out ravines in the hill-side, and gradually uniting merge into the valleys of small streams flowing to the Colne or Thames. At three points in the range, where the chalk is soft, ancient rivers have worn down the ridge sufficiently to provide easy passes on a gravel bed from the London side to the Vale. The northernmost and flattest enters the hills at Watford, passes Berkhampstead, and emerges near Tring. The convenience of this passage was noted by the Romans, who drove their Akeman Street right through it to Aylesbury and on to Cirencester, and its course was followed by the Grand Junction canal, which crossed its gentle gradients with no undue expenditure in locks—the only water to penetrate the Chiltern chain. At a later date the same route was taken by the London and North Western railway, and, with the help of a by-pass round Watford, the old Akeman Street still does duty as a main arterial highway. The second pass runs between great headlands at Wendover; four miles to the south it strikes the springs of the Misbourne and accompanies the stream downwards by Amersham and the Chalfonts to the Colne at Uxbridge. Its road was followed by Leland in the reign of King Henry VIII and by many an eighteenth-century traveller. Its railway, jointly owned by the Metropolitan and Great Central companies, came in 1892. The third pass is the widest, but points in a direction that renders it of less service to London. It follows an offshoot of the High Wycombe Valley past Bradenham to reach the Vale at Princes Risborough between the upstanding bluff of Bledlow Ridge and the hills of Whiteleaf. Its railway used to serve only the country districts from High Wycombe to Aylesbury, Oxford and Watlington, but, with the coming of a new direct line from London through Beaconsfield, it has developed into a fast route to Birmingham. South of this the ridge runs unbroken to the Thames, and the straight roads from London to Oxford by Nettlebed and by Stokenchurch have to climb to the summit and descend the precipitous escarpment.

These passes have maintained rather than destroyed the

quietude of the country through which they run. They serve as useful outlets for the vapours of the Great City, as chimneys save a house from smuts, and have hitherto concentrated the through traffic, and with it the less amiable products of civilization, into defined and narrow channels. Along the lines of the great roads and railways, and, in patches, on all the slopes nearest London, many changes have come in recent years—leafy lanes transformed into wide, straight, hedgeless highways, pleasant fields yielded up to bricks and mortar. But the discretion of some of the landowners in selecting sites for building, coupled with the natural configuration of the ground, has done a great deal to localize the trouble: much can be tucked away unseen in these deep hollows or beneath the sheltering canopy of beechwoods. Even where new towns have sprung up almost in the night, a few steps from these centres of population will often lead one into unspoilt English country. As one moves away toward the topmost ridge, the valleys divide and subdivide into lesser and lesser valleys; above the town of Chesham the valley of the Chess breaks up into seven, and a dozen hollows unite to form the long vale of Hughenden, which in turn becomes a feeder of the Wye Valley at Wycombe. Near the summit the little valleys lie closely packed, separated one from another by narrow razor-backed ridges, each as secluded and self-contained as a cell in a Trappist monastery. A revolution might wreck the peace of Upper North Dean, while Bryants Bottom half a mile away slept soundly in its beds. Here the seeker after seclusion has no longer need to pick his way, and in numberless walks within a limited area can rarely fail to light on something new. Yet from these solitary spurs on any clear moonless night one can see reflected on the clouds the dancing flames of London.

Such a country, with its lonely struggles against an unaccommodating Nature and its bracing nip of upland air, leads to independent thinking and strong convictions. It was a stronghold of Lollards, who braved the tortures of mediæval orthodoxy, and after them of Quakers. Every movement against oppression has here found its stoutest champions. Its quietude is not the kind that generates sloth, but rather gives rest before battle. When the generosity of Lord and Lady Lee converted the old manor house of Chequers into a country retreat for prime ministers, they were only giving permanence to a long-established tradition: four Prime Ministers—Shelburne, Portland, Grenville, Beaconsfield—to say nothing of other statesmen of the calibre of Penn, or Burke, or Lyndhurst, had already tested the recuperative powers of the district. Many a poet has found it, but they mostly carolled on the lower slopes. Shelley sought inspiration beneath the many weirs of Hurley; Gray haunted the woods of Burnham and Stoke Poges; and Milton found a temporary home in his " pretty box " beside the Misbourne. Waller's courtly muse had little of the country note. The waterless summits were reserved for Rupert Brooke, who looked down from the escarpment on " the slumbering Midland plain," found " laughter and inn fires " at the " Pink and Lily," and turned homeward through " the dead leaves in the lane."

It is to me a country of many and varied interests apart from its obvious beauty; and if any one should object that no great events of national importance have happened within it, I would answer that, if Waterloo was won on the playing fields of Eton, Pennsylvania was founded in the narrow lanes and woodlands between Rickmansworth and Jordans. Beneath the trees of Great Hampden were set the limits of constitutional monarchy; and from Burke's home at Beaconsfield came the clarion call for sympathy with the American colonists. On the lawns of Hughenden the " Young England " party was born: " We live in an age when to be young and to be indifferent can be no longer synonymous. We must prepare for the coming hour. The claims of the Future are represented by suffering millions, and the Youth of a Nation are the Trustees of Posterity."

In the chapters that follow I propose to guide you by devious routes to all these places, but the woodland hollows where we shall ramble hold many curious things besides unknown to history-books. We will set out from the

railway passes or the main highways—one day from Berkhampstead or Gerrards Cross, on others from Wycombe
or Beaconsfield, from Great Missenden or Henley—and
strike for the open country. Some days we will walk
among great houses, on others we will follow hidden
valleys, where little Norman churches rise from ancient
villages. Our only aim will be to come to something
beautiful or interesting by the most congenial path.
Although this country has more homogeneity than any of
the three counties into which we shall pursue our quest,
yet it lacks any geographical name or limits. We cannot
rule off its boundaries by lines of latitude and longitude like
an American state. Still less can we leave them to a plebis-
cite, like the League of Nations: for it is a subtle quality
we seek, not the opinions of a quantity of mixed people.
The question of the boundaries, then, *solvitur ambulando*.
We can turn back when the scent grows cold, and skip
a little, casting forward, if the scent grows patchy. And,
for a name, we call our streets after great men: can we
do better for our newly-created country? Of all the
great men whose names are associated with it, I feel none
to be more typical of its quality than William Penn. His
simple grave in the little burial-place at Jordans has for
two centuries drawn more pilgrims than any other Chiltern shrine: many, coming from overseas, have here made
their first acquaintance with quiet English country. As
the prophets of old withdrew into the desert for a space
before entering on some great mission, so Penn retired for
a time from fickle crowds and the worries of public life
into this quiet sanctuary. In many a homestead still
standing hereabouts he was welcomed by his humbler
friends when the great world treated him with scorn.
Here he dreamed his dreams, which, in the face of continuous opposition, he made at last come true. We will
call it " The Penn Country." It is possible that its centre
may have shifted a little to-day: that seekers after peace
and freedom would now choose a harbour of refuge a
little more remote from modern development. But the
quality of the whole country we shall traverse seems to
have something of a Quakerish air, both in its quietude

and unostentatious comeliness, and also in its old-fashioned difference from the common run.

To-day the Penn Country is still a sanctuary: a place of quiet beauty, not far from London, where those who love such things can find a patch of genuine country England. But what of to-morrow? In certain parts building has increased during recent years with extraordinary rapidity. The figures speak for themselves. Between 1901 and 1921 the population of Amersham rose from 2674 to 4421, of Chesham Bois from 767 to 1792; and, nearer Jordans, we have Chalfont St. Peters, 1402 to 4183; Chalfont St. Giles, 1367 to 2074; and Gerrards Cross, 552 to 2208. Beaconsfield has practically doubled the area of its houses, and the same increase is apparent along the slopes by Burnham and Farnham Royal, and throughout the Misbourne valley. And the invasion still goes on. Where the new building has been concentrated in well-sited and well-planned little towns or villages, the effect on the district at large is small: it is the isolated settlements spread about the country, the thin rows of bungalows along the roads, that threaten its charm. A single garish villa can banish the silence and mystery from a whole valley.

There is a sound moral in the story of " Builder " Boyle, fourth Earl of Burlington, who erected Burlington House in what is now Piccadilly for his London home. When his friends asked him why he built it so far out of town, he answered that he did not wish to have any other house beyond him. Attempts to " return to nature," to build a rustic cottage out of sight of other habitations and live " the world forgetting, by the world forgot," are equally futile in the Chilterns. Once one house comes, others follow. The owner, having sold a corner of a field for building, finds the whole rated as building land, and recoups himself by selling more. Nor is the flush of sentiment that leads to such excursions always conducive to well-considered design. I know of one devoted couple who adorned their first little nest on the pattern of the Blackpool boarding-house where they spent their honeymoon: and the staring pink-roofed bungalow constantly recurs, devastating some peaceful scene, where a simple well-proportioned cottage, built of the soft-faced brick that grows mellow with age, might pass unnoticed. When the sentimental invader, wearied by abortive hunts for servants and the lack of the common conveniences of civilized communities, retires defeated to the town whence he came, the wound in our sanctuary remains behind.

There is another particularly unpleasant consequence of this hermitage type of settlement. Such houses lie outside the collecting area of Council refuse-carts: and, wherever they appear, woods and commons around them become defiled by an ever-extending ring of old tins, broken crockery, and anything else unpleasant that cannot readily be burnt. The hermits are not the only offenders. Many a Chiltern common is thus defaced. When you visit it in summer, much is hidden by fronds of bracken: but if you saw it in the winter, you would never wish to picnic there again. There are, of course, many brilliant exceptions. The glorious wooded hills near Hambleden, where all may ramble, I have always found spotless. At the entrance is a notice-board informing the ignorant and warning the thoughtless of what must or must not be done if the place is to keep the same charm for the next-comer: and, at the foot, " By order of the Lord of the Manor." This form, somehow, seems to be more generally respected than the edicts of a local council or even the appeals of the National Trust. Almost always, where the common lands are noticeably clean, I find some resident lord of the manor owning the property about them. Perhaps the cause is partly psychological. A definite anthropomorphic presence has a greater reality to men's minds than a council that changes its spots at each election or a vague abstraction with an office in London; but I am sure that the tact and vigilance exercised day by day, week by week, by many a squire have a more enduring influence for good than the spasmodic efforts of well-intentioned societies.

These threatening evils have not yet eaten deeply into the Penn country: little has been done that is irremediable. But it is necessary to check in time tendencies which, if allowed to spread and gather force, might eventually destroy a very precious heritage. To-day we have miles of glorious open country before us, hallowed by the memories of great men, and it may still be saved for future generations. Surely an age that has preserved so many sanctuaries for birds and savage beasts will not deny a sanctuary to man.

CHAPTER II

WE ENTER THE PENN COUNTRY

" 1671. 12th month, 7th day.—Our Friend William
Penn of Walthamstow in ye County of Essex & Gulielma
Maria Springett of Tilerend-Green in ye parish of Penn
in ye County of Bucks proposed their intentions of Marriage at ye Monthly Meetting at Hunger Hill."

" 1672. 1st month, 6th day.—They received ye answer
wch was ye consent and approbation of ye Meetting."

" 1672. 2nd month, 4th day.—They took each other in
Marriage at Chorlewood at a farmhouse called Kings
where friends Meetting was then kept being in ye parish
of Rickmansworth in ye County of Hertford." [1]

SO run the entries copied into the diary of Mistress
Rebekah Butterfield which gives us so much interesting information about the early history of the
Chiltern Quakers. We shall visit her home at Stone Dean
when we go to Jordans; but in that William Penn, in
marrying Guli Springett, may be said to have also married what we call the Penn Country, Chorleywood is a
fitting spot from which to start upon our Chiltern pilgrimage. Passengers from London by the Metropolitan
and Great Central Railway know it well as the only place
that presents a genuine Chiltern common to their eyes.
Passing with relief from the curious experiments of the
builders of Greater Rickmansworth into a refreshing wood

[1] The early Quakers refused to use the customary pagan names for
the months and days of the week. As New Year's Day, by the
Old Style of reckoning, fell in March, the 12th month was February.
When Rebekah Butterfield dates an incident " 10–22–1 " she means
the 22nd day of the 10th month (December) being the first day of
the week (Sunday).

9

of pines and larches, the traveller emerges to see, on his right, a rising bank of smooth green downland crowned with a blaze of flaming gorse which falls in irregular patches down the slope.   Bounded on one side by the main road from London, on the other by the railway, Chorleywood Common has still contrived to retain its rural charm.   Only the other day I flushed a covey of partridges among its bracken. The old village, which mostly lies about its north-east corner, was a noted head-quarters of the early Quakers: in a house across the road from the modern church, during its occupation by the Wilson family, they held their meetings for many a year, and their little graveyard lies beside it.   When the church-yard of the new parish was consecrated, the bishop crossed the road to bestow a blessing upon their last resting-place.

The new town, running up the opposite hill beyond the railway, is less inviting, but, though our road lies in that direction, we can avoid the greater part of it if we visit first the house where William Penn was married.   We shall find it changed both in name and in appearance. When I asked the way to King's Farm at Chorleywood Station, they were frankly puzzled, and then somebody wondered if I meant *Edward* King's farm.   It was only after considerable explanation that I discovered that the house I sought was now King John's Farm.   The King family has long flourished in the district, and it is not impossible that some early Edward King gave the place its old title; but a vague tradition connects the house with a royal hunting-box, and the name has presumably been lengthened to give substance to this version.   There is nothing regal about the simple little building of which a photograph appears in Mr. Summers' informative book, *Memories of Jordans and the Chalfonts,* published in 1895; and it was for this house that I was looking as I followed my directions.   It lies about half a mile away, and the best way to find it is to turn to the right outside the station, cross the next bridge over the railway, and, at the bottom of the hill, take a footpath on the left of the road which runs up a steep slope to a group of trees. Turning right in the lane at the top, we find it hiding behind the spinney at a corner formed by a side road leading to Rickmansworth, where Penn and his bride spent the first years of their married life. But the present house bears no resemblance to the photograph: it is indeed our first introduction to the " converted " farm-houses of which we shall meet many on our rambles. The conversion has here been drastic. King John's Farm, to-day, is a well-executed reproduction of a Jacobean manor-house with much black oak about its gables, such as one meets in Herefordshire or Shropshire. It must be four times the size of the original building. The elaborate weathercock on its topmost ridge of roof bears the initials of William Penn, but one thinks, at first, that the farm he knew must be entirely enclosed within, like the little tabernacle of St. Francis in the great church below Assisi hill. Closer inspection of the back wall, facing the road, reveals patches of old brick and close perpendicular beams, as shown in Mr. Summers' photograph, but only a very picturesque old barn remains to justify the name of " Farm."

We continue on the way by which we came, enjoying fine views of common and woodland across the valley on the right, and, where the lane bends near the school, go forward by a footpath into the main road running up-hill from the station. We turn to the left, and soon, where the road forks, bear to the right. We are now fairly on our road to the Chalfonts, crossing the ridge dividing the Misbourne valley from the dry bottom that descends from Chalfont Road station to the Colne below Rickmansworth. We enter a pleasant rolling country to which nature has given no particular character of its own. It lacks the abruptness of the upper Chilterns, the sudden turnings that bring an unexpected view or the deep hidden valleys into which we fall before we see them. But the beechwoods that close our view on every side are always a delight, dressing their windows afresh with each succeeding season. The ridge is singularly un-spoilt by its great increase of population. The road we follow is bordered by private parks, but the newer houses away on either side are well-placed among the woods, and the lesser houses cluster in groups instead of spreading for miles along the road. We start with Beechwood Park upon our left, and we can cut off a corner pleasantly by following a footpath from its gate. Where the road beyond is joined by another from Chalfont Road Station we bear to the left, with the park of The Vache upon our right. The Vache is a very ancient manor-house; though considerably restored, it still retains the characteristics shared by similar mansions in the Chilterns: a well-proportioned house of plain stone, economical of ornament and depending for its charm upon its situation, woods and avenues. Clever people who know French have decided that it was a noted dairy-farm in the days of the Plantagenets, but the ancient family named de la Vache, who then inhabited it, may well have kept their cows in Normandy before they came to occupy this pleasant Chiltern slope. The property passed later on Thomas Fleetwood, Queen Elizabeth's Master of the Mint, whose family occupied many seats in the county, and was held by his descendants till George Fleetwood, one of the judges of King Charles I, was evicted after the Restoration. After this it was owned by many families. It was first granted to the Duke of York, from whom it passed to Sir Thomas Clayton, a Justice of the Peace who appears in Quaker records as a zealous persecutor of Friends. By marriage the estate came soon afterwards to Francis Hare, Bishop of Chichester, who had held the exacting post of chaplain to the great Duke of Marlborough and had accompanied him at the battles of Blenheim and Ramillies. A striking feature was added to the grounds by a bluff Yorkshire sailor, Admiral Sir Hugh Palliser, who bought The Vache in 1771 after his bitter quarrel with Admiral Keppel. Palliser had been the first commander to recommend James Cook, the celebrated explorer, for promotion in the Navy, and, when he was appointed Governor of Newfoundland, selected Cook as his marine surveyor to make charts of the coast. The friendship continued in later life: Cook named a newly-discovered island " Ile Vache "; and, after the explorer's murder, Palliser set up an elaborate monument to him in his park. On an artificial mound, surrounded by a moat, he erected a round tower. A staircase gives access to the flat roof, where an excellent view of the house and its woods may be obtained. On the floor below, beneath this canopy, a model of the globe stands on a pedestal, with a long inscription in which, while praising his dead friend, the irascible old sailor inserted a hit at the controversialists who had held that there must be a great Antarctic continent in order to balance the mass of land known to exist in the northern hemisphere.

" Traveller! " (he wrote), "contemplate, admire, revere and emulate this great master in his profession whose skill and labours have enlarged natural philosophy, have extended nautical science, and have disclosed the long-concealed and admirable arrangement of the Almighty in the formation of the globe and, at the same time, the arrogance of mortals in presuming to account by their speculations for the laws by which He was pleased to create it. . . . It is now discovered beyond all doubt that the same Great Being who created the Universe by his fiat, by the same ordained our earth to keep a just poise without a corresponding Southern Continent, and it does so."

The entrance to The Vache is in the road that descends into the valley at Chalfont St. Giles; but we will keep on the hill a little longer and bear to the left to visit Chalfont St. Peter. From the old home of a Master of the Mint we pass at once to the park and house constructed by a Georgian banker. The woods of Newland Park are on our left and we follow the fence as far as the entrance gateway through which we have a good view of the long drive leading to the mansion. Abraham Newland, who built the house and gave it his name, was a very well-known man in his day—so much so that he became the hero of a popular song written by the younger Charles Dibdin, son of the author of *Tom Bowling*. After thirty years' service in the Bank of England he became its chief cashier in 1778. At that time all bank-notes were signed by hand, and, since his autograph appeared upon them, five-pound notes were popularly known as " Newlands," just as the currency notes of the Great War were christened " Bradburys." The avenue within the park is continued across the road by a double line of dark firs, and we turn down the lane that runs between them to regain the lower road which we might have followed at a previous turn. We come out opposite Ashwells Farm, a converted farm-house of the best type. No liberties have been taken with its outside appearance. It still remains a fine old Chiltern homestead with lattice windows; great gables of brick and timber point in all directions, and black barns of different shapes leaning at different angles sit about it on either side. Gay flower-beds decorate the old farmyard; a wistaria twines about a barn, but, beyond this, the " conversion " has been all inside.

Following the straight road forward past a few new houses and chicken-farms we come to one of those curious things that are always cropping up in the Chilterns. A great obelisk rises by the left side of the lane some sixty feet high, projecting far above the trees and houses around it and forming a conspicuous object when seen from the far side of the Misbourne valley. It is built of flints, with corners of brick to strengthen the topmost point, and towards the bottom a panel with inscription is inserted. This inscription is headed by the date 1788: pointing fingers indicate that the road leads one way to Newland I Mile III furlongs, and to Chesham VII Miles, and the other way to Denham IV Miles, to Uxbridge VI, and to London XXI. In the centre is the information that it was erected by Sir Henry Gott and repaired in 1879 by Mr. W. Brown. But as to its origin, use or meaning there is not a word. It stands at no important crossway where a traveller might need guidance, and the houses near so obviously belong to a later date that the column must have been erected far from any human habitation. Inquiry fails to elicit any certain information: the experts differ. The guide-books tell you that King George III was hunting here and that the obelisk marks the spot where he was present at the death of a stag. The very tactlessness of the proceeding condemns the story. Who would erect a trophy on a cricket-ground where some royal amateur had made a run? I cling to the local version that you may hear from the lips of the rude forefathers of the hamlet in the " Greyhound " or the " Pheasant." King George was certainly hunting, but he got lost and separated from his attendants in a sudden fog. After much aimless wandering he here met a yokel and made inquiries as to his whereabouts. The man pointed vaguely in the mist to inform him that " Peter's lies down there, and Giles's over yonder." " But what is *this* place? " asked the impatient monarch. " This baint no place at all, not rightly," was the answer. " Well," said the King, " we shall have to make it a place: let's put up a monument." And there the monument stands to-day to prove the truth of the story.

Passing the obelisk we bear to the right down a road marked Chesham Lane, and, descending Gravel Hill, we find ourselves at no great distance from the village of Chalfont St. Peter. The big house of the place lies on the far side of the village and we will pass through to visit it first: it is the furthest point we shall visit towards London. Within recent years great changes have fallen upon this lower valley. The gentle slopes that rise to an elevation of some 200 feet on the eastern side are in process of development as the " Chalfont Heights Estate," and on the opposite hill a great new town covers a solid square mile from here to Gerrards Cross station. The new Gerrards Cross has been christened by a friendly advertiser " The Brighton of Bucks," and we may leave it at that. Meanwhile we must feel all gratitude to the enterprising hotel company that has taken over the old mansion and rescued some 300 acres of its glorious park from imminent destruction.

The house is best known through its connection with Horace Walpole, the entertaining, if spiteful, letter-writer and amateur of sham Gothic architecture, for here lived Colonel Charles Churchill who married Walpole's sister, Lady Maria. It has often been stated that Churchill built

it, but the house obviously is older in origin, and many
trees of astonishing girth, planted for ornamental purposes about the drive, must already have grown old
when the Lady Maria was a bride. Horace Walpole himself refutes the legend. He always writes the place
" Chaffont," which gives what is still the local pronuncia-
tion. " Last week," he writes in 1755, soon after the
Churchill occupation, " we were at my sister's, at Chaffont in Buckinghamshire, to see what we could make of
it; but it wants so much of everything, and would require
so much more of an inventionary of five thousand pounds,
that we decided nothing, except that Mr. Chute has designed the prettiest house in the world for them." One is
grateful that the inventionary of five thousand pounds
would go no farther. Horace Walpole and Chute would
have pulled the whole place down and started afresh. But
architect-archæologists maintain that much of the old red-
brick building exists beneath the covering of stucco, and
it is an interesting exercise to try to pick out the earlier
from the later portions. The west front where the main
entrance lies is pure Strawberry Hill Gothic, with its toy
turrets and unnecessary ornament, but on the other sides
it is not impossible to think away the conceits which
Horace Walpole thrust upon his sister and picture a square
red house something after the pattern of a lesser Hampton
Court. The widening of the Misbourne to form a narrow
lake below the house would also follow the Walpole tradition, but the outlines of old fishponds, still visible in the
park, are of indubitably mediæval pattern. The beautiful
texture and colour of the old bricks may be seen in the
walls that enclose the garden behind. Within them Sir
Edwin Lutyens has lately constructed an Italian garden of
great beauty, with basins of running water down the
middle and clipped yews on either side. A glass building
like an orangery projects from the wall at the end—a
portion of the club-house of the Chalfont Park Golf Club
which lies behind: a peaceful spot to which a member
can retire from the field of battle and feel more philo-
sophical about that foozle at the sixteenth. Their 18-hole
course on the eastern slopes of the valley and the 9-hole

course near the hotel are perhaps the best guarantee of the future integrity of the Park; for to steal a hole from a golf-course would to-day rouse greater opposition than to rob Jordans of all its quietude.

We retrace our steps down the long drive leading towards Chalfont St. Peter, and till we pass through the gate great trees on our left shelter the park from the outer world. The village streets have changed not at all, and the little stream, crossed by a bridge near the church, forms a pleasant feature; but the approach from this side is lamentable. The houses on the hill towards Gerrards Cross are not unpleasing: one may regret the loss of open country, but, since new settlements must be made, the plateau above is as good a place as any. But along the road below bungalows of startling design and colouring, mixed with immense advertisements of land speculators, unnecessarily accentuate the discord between new buildings and the old village behind. Surely Beaconsfield and Amersham planned more wisely in separating their new towns from the old.

At the entrance to the village street we pass on the left the grounds of The Grange, a house that played an important part in the early history of the Chiltern Quakers. The Grange has to-day little sign of seventeenth-century workmanship. It has seen many strange vicissitudes. After a short life as a residential hotel it has lately become a Convent school; and at a much earlier date it passed from that worthy Quaker family, the Peningtons, to become the temporary abode of Judge Jeffreys. Jeffreys lived in several houses hereabouts while he was rebuilding Bulstrode, and he is said to have erected the Greyhound Inn. This pleasant old building, which sits sideways to face the traveller from London, must be set to the credit side of his account against the Bloody Assizes. Its left wing, resting on the street, is pierced by a narrow archway, leading to the yard, that must have tested the skill of the old stage-coachmen; and its right wall has its foundations on an island in the Misbourne, which partly runs beneath the house. At the present time it possesses an intelligent parrot that sits in the bar-parlour and scrutinizes each

2

new-comer from head to foot; if not quite satisfied, it emits a sad but firm " Good-bye! "

But our interest in Chalfont Grange lies mainly in the period before Jeffreys. Here lived Isaac Penington the elder, sometime Lord Mayor of London and Lieutenant of the Tower. He was a violent Republican and Presbyterian, and presented the famous " Root and Branch " petition for the abolition of all bishops. This and his attitude at the King's trial made him a marked man at the Restoration. His property was sequestrated; imprisonment in the Tower hastened his death, and he passes out of our story. But some years before this he had handed over the Grange to his son Isaac, after the latter's marriage to Lady Springett, who had lost her first husband at twenty years of age. Isaac Penington the younger, and all his family, became early adherents of George Fox, and their Quaker principles caused an estrangement with the elder Penington; as they were also known to be opposed to his republican sentiments, they were allowed to remain for some years on sufferance at The Grange, and the house became an important headquarters of the Society of Friends. Many letters of the Peningtons have been preserved which throw interesting sidelights upon those troubled times, but still more informative is the *Autobiography* of Thomas Ellwood, who had first known Mrs. Penington at a very tender age. Thomas was the son of Walter Ellwood, the squire of the little village of Crowell that lies beneath the Chiltern escarpment not far from Thame; and the story of his first meeting with Gulielma Springett, the future wife of William Penn, is best told in his own words.

" In my very Infancy," he writes, " when I was but about two Years old, I was carried to *London*. For the Civil War, between King and Parliament, breaking then forth, my Father, who favoured the Parliament-side, though he took not up Arms, not holding himself safe at his Country Habitation, which lay too near some Garrisons of the King's, betook himself to *London*, that City then holding for the Parliament. . . . In this time my Parents contracted an Acquaintance and intimate Friendship with the Lady Springett, who being then the widow of Sir *William Springett,* who died in the Parliament Service, was afterwards the Wife of *Isaac Penington,* eldest Son of Alderman *Penington* of *London.* And this Friendship devolving from the Parents to the Children, I became an early and particular Play-fellow of her Daughter *Gulielma,* being admitted, as such, to ride with her in her little Coach, drawn by her Footman about *Lincolns-Inn-Fields.*" After the surrender of Oxford the Ellwoods returned to Crowell, but their acquaintance was kept up with Lady Springett. Mrs. Ellwood had died: but the squire and his son Thomas were early visitors at The Grange.

" I mentioned before," writes Thomas, " that during my Father's Abode in *London,* in the time of the Civil Wars, he contracted a Friendship with the Lady *Springett,* then a Widow, and afterwards married to Isaac Penington, Esq; to continue which, he sometimes visited them at their Country Lodgings, as at *Datchet,* and at *Causham* [Caversham] *Lodge* near Reading. And having heard that they were to come to live upon their own Estate at *Chalfont* in *Buckinghamshire,* about fifteen Miles from *Crowell,* he went one Day to visit them there, and to return at Night, taking me with him.

" But very much surprized we were, when, being come thither, we first heard, then found, they were become *Quakers*; a people we had no Knowledge of, and a Name we had, till then, scarce heard of.

" So great a Change from a free, debonair and courtly sort of Behaviour, which we formerly had found them in, to so strict a Gravity as they now received us with, did not a little amuse us, and disappoint our Expectation of such a pleasant Visit as we used to have, and had now promised ourselves. Nor could my Father have any Opportunity, by a private Conference with them, to understand the Ground and Occasion of this Change, there being some other Strangers with them (related to *Isaac Penington*) who came that morning from *London* to visit them also.

" For my part I sought, and at length found Means to cast myself into the Company of the Daughter, whom I found gathering some Flowers in the Garden, attended by her Maid who was also a *Quaker*.   But when I addressed myself to her after my accustomed Manner, with Intention to engage her in some Discourse, which might introduce Conversation, on the Foot of our former Acquaintance; though she treated me with a courteous Mein, yet, as young as she was, the Gravity of her Look and Behaviour struck such an Awe upon me, that I found myself not so much Master of myself as to pursue any further Converse with her.   Wherefore asking Pardon for my Boldness in having intruded myself into her private Walks, I withdrew, not without some Disorder (as I thought at least) of Mind.

" We staid Dinner, which was very handsome, and lacked nothing to recommend it to me but the want of Mirth and pleasant Discourse, which we could neither have with them, nor, by reason of them, with one another amongst ourselves; the Weightiness that was upon their Spirits and Countenances keeping down the Lightness that would have been up in us.   We staid notwithstanding till the rest of the Company took Leave of them, and then we also, doing the same, returned, not greatly satisfied with our Journey, nor knowing what in particular to find Fault with . . ."

Nevertheless the Ellwoods were interested: they paid a second visit, this time of some days' duration and accompanied the Penington family to a Quaker Meeting held at The Grove, which stands among trees above the valley at the other side of the village.   Thomas Ellwood, then a young man of twenty, at once determined to join the Society of Friends and, like Isaac Penington before him and William Penn after, met with strong opposition from his father.   The squire was particularly annoyed by his son wearing a hat in his presence and attending Quaker meetings; he destroyed his hats, beat him with a cane, took away his money, and tried to confine him in the house, but eventually, finding all opposition useless, let the youth go his own way and soon retired to London. Thomas, for his part, underwent every form of persecution to which Quakers were then liable: he was arrested repeatedly for no particular reason and saw the inside of Newgate and Bridewell in London as well as of the local gaols at Wycombe and Aylesbury. The Grange at Chalfont became a second home where he was always welcome; and, when young Ellwood expressed a wish to improve his education, it was Penington who found him a tutor in London, and that tutor was John Milton. Ellwood read Latin books to the blind poet and received instruction in return.

When Ellwood returned from London in 1662, he became a regular inmate of The Grange, for Isaac Penington engaged him as tutor to his young children. He also came after a time to help in business affairs, journeying to Kent to collect rents from Mary Penington's estates in that county, and took charge of the whole family during Penington's long and frequent imprisonments. In the cultured atmosphere of The Grange he met many leaders of the Society; among them were George Fox himself and Thomas Loe of Oxford, who first influenced William Penn in his undergraduate days, and, meeting him again in Ireland in 1665, won over the polished courtier to the Quaker cause. All this time Thomas Ellwood was thrown into the closest intimacy with Gulielma Springett, Isaac's stepdaughter, and frequently escorted her on horseback when she went to visit relatives and friends. Reading between the lines of his story, one cannot doubt that Thomas was touched by her charm and beauty. All who knew her spoke well of her. Sober old Joseph Besse, in writing of William Penn's marriage, describes his bride as " a Young Woman, whom a Virtuous Disposition, joyn'd to a Comely Personage, render'd well accomplished." Penn's eulogy upon her at her death comes straight from the heart, and succeeding ages have looked upon her as the ideal of Quaker womanhood. The testimony of Thomas Ellwood, her lifelong friend, is worth quoting:

" While I thus remained in this Family, various suspicions arose in the Minds of some concerning me, with respect to *Mary Penington's* daughter *Guli*. For she having now arrived to a marriageable Age, and being in all respects a very desirable Woman (whether regard was had to her outward Person, which wanted nothing to render her compleatly comely; or to the Endowments of her Mind, which were in every way extraordinary, and highly obliging; or to her outward Fortune, which was fair, and which with some hath not the last, nor the least Place in Consideration) she was openly and secretly sought and solicited by many, and some of them almost of every Rank and Condition; Good and Bad, Rich and Poor, Friend and Foe. To whom, in their respective Turns (till he at length came, for whom she was reserved) she carried herself with so much Evenness of Temper, such courteous Freedom, guarded with the strictest Modesty, that as it gave Encouragement, or ground of Hopes to none, so did it neither administer any matter of Offence, or just Cause of Complaint to any.

" But such as were thus either engaged for themselves, or desirous to make themselves Advocates for others, could not, I observed, but look upon me with an Eye of Jealousy and Fear, that I would improve the Opportunities I had, by frequent and familiar Conversation with her, to my own Advantage, in working myself into her good Opinion and Favour, to the Ruin of their Pretences. According, therefore, to the several Kinds and Degrees of their Fears of me, they suggested to her Parents their ill Surmises against me."

The Peningtons trusted Ellwood completely and he proved worthy of their confidence. " I governed myself," he writes, " in a free, yet respectful Carriage towards her, that I thereby both preserved a fair Reputation with my Friends, and enjoyed as much of her Favour and Kindness, in a virtuous and firm Friendship, as was fit for her to shew, or for me to seek." Ellwood remained with the family till, in 1669, he married Mary Ellis, and went to live at Hunger Hill. But before this the hospitable home at The Grange was broken up. In 1665, when Isaac Penington was in Aylesbury gaol, the suspended sentence

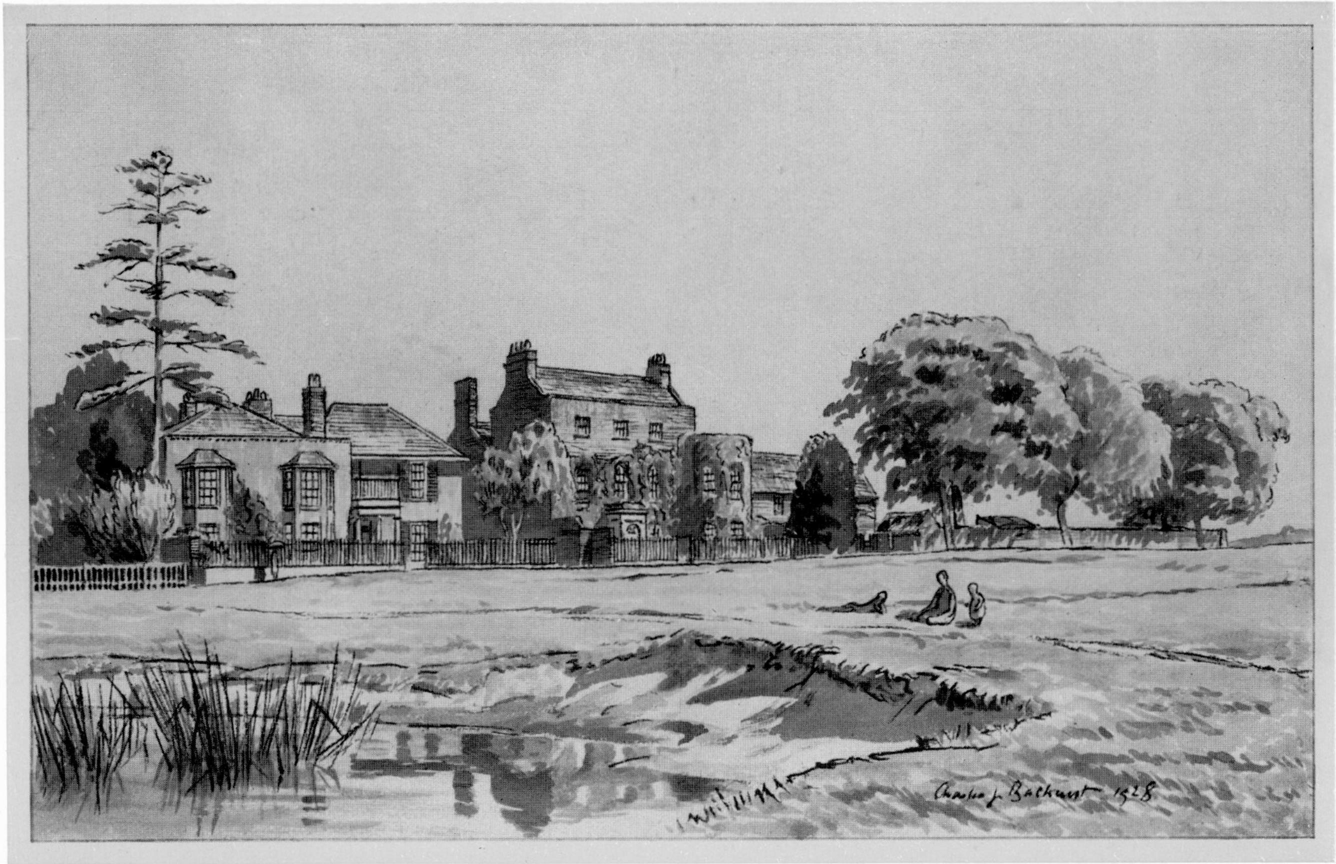

AT GERRARD'S CROSS.

of ejectment was put into force. Mary Penington and her children were left homeless, and Ellwood escorted them first to Aylesbury, then to Bottrells Farm near Chalfont St. Giles, and finally to Amersham. William Penn—" he for whom she was reserved "—therefore never met Gulielma at The Grange: it was at Amersham that he courted her, and at Thomas Ellwood's house that their proposal of marriage was submitted to the Meeting.

We leave this pleasant circle with regret, but we shall meet most of them again in various houses to which the storm of persecution blew them, and find them all re-united in the little burial-ground at Jordans. We turn the next corner to the left, in the middle of the village, and are soon ascending the little triangular common of Gold Hill. In spite of the mass of recent building around, the common is little changed, for its inner rim was established before the deluge. There are good houses along the cross-road at the top, and a picturesque row of cottages is backed by the trees of The Grange on our left. The road to the right would lead us straight by Welders Lane to Jordans; but we have tramped enough for the day and make to the left for Gerrards Cross Station. The more direct road running from the gates of Chalfont Park is bordered by garden palings all the way; but taking this route we pass quickly from Gold Hill to Austenwood Common, which, if its new surroundings give it something of the air of a caged bird, displays a grateful stretch of gorse upon our right, with the same old cottage, with its red brick chimney and roof of mellow tiles all smothered in clematis, standing as picturesquely in its midst as it did with fields around it. Nearer the station we enter a street precisely the same as those we see from the train in London suburbs. It crosses the railway, which here runs through a deep cutting, and one follows it on out of curiosity to see how far this tide of invasion has pene-trated. But within a few hundred yards the end comes suddenly, and we emerge on Gerrards Cross Common, bordering the Oxford Road, to find it quite unchanged from the days when Gerrards Cross was two inns, a score of houses, and an eccentric church. One can still picture

the highwaymen riding through the gorse—Jack
Shrimpton from Penn or the Irishman MacQueer—and
understand why Captain Mayne Reid settled here to find
inspiration for *The Scalp Hunters, The Headless Horseman,* and other absorbing tales that thrilled our school-
days. Round to the right, opposite the great gates of
Bulstrode Park, was a little corner that always gave me
pleasure, where a rounded duckpond reflected a group of
comfortable houses beyond. The scene has altered not at
all; the same ducks might still be rippling its surface. The
houses are of no remote antiquity: they recall the leisured
times of Jane Austen rather than the troubled days of
Guli Penn. But Mr. Bathurst's drawing testifies to the
repose and peacefulness of the spot. And this is a feature
we shall constantly find in the Penn Country. Here, on
its lower slopes, old winding lanes are being flattened into
streets, green fields devoured by bricks and mortar. But
within a stone's throw of these new centres of population
one has only to turn a corner to find some oasis like this,
and enter the land of ancient peace where Penn shaped
his dreams of distant settlements, and many another
famous in his generation has since come to seek repose
after toil or to gather new strength for the battle.

CHAPTER III

TO JORDANS AND BEYOND

IT is not so long ago that a visit to Jordans was something of a pilgrimage, not only (as now) in spirit, but in the difficulties that attended it. It lay far from any railway and away from any main road; and early visitors from every direction came through miles of unspoilt country. They travelled by twisting lanes or open bridle-paths that had changed but little since William and Gulielma Penn rode over from Rickmansworth to meeting; and, by whatever way they came, they were bound to arrive at this humble Quaker shrine, venerated by thousands on both sides of the world, with minds attuned to appreciate its restful charm.

Jordans itself—the little meeting-house with the three houses around that have helped it to make history—still enjoys its old quietude, though its peacefulness is seriously threatened by modern developments. But its approaches are already entirely altered. A red ring of suburbs encircles Chalfont St. Peters; the cross-roads at Chalfont St. Giles is a garish wilderness of advertisements; and off-shoots of the new Beaconsfield are creeping near Seer Green. The neighbouring station of Seer Green Halt is an impossible approach: vast hoardings offering building sites hit you in the face as you emerge. I maintain that to-day the best way to come to Jordans is to walk from Gerrards Cross Station. We must pick our way at first with some care, in order that we may strike the right footpath when the houses end.

Let us start then, in the face of all probabilities, along the cinder-track that follows the edge of the railway-cutting on its northern side; where the path ends at a footbridge we turn right into Bull Lane, and follow it to the left. At the next fork we bear to the left again by Maltmans Lane, which leads to what was once the hamlet of Maltmans Green, but is, at the moment, the furthest outpost of Gerrards Cross. We reach a sharp turn to the right marked " Dangerous Bend," but avoid the obvious footpath that leads straight forward; and, braving the peril round the corner, take another path that leaves the lane to the left near Maltmans Green school and can be seen following the left side of a hedgerow in the open fields beyond. At Maltmans Green lived old William Grimsdale, the Quaker, who became one of the first trustees of Jordans Meeting-house when it was erected in 1688. By this same path must he have often walked to watch the building rise brick by brick in its sequestered hollow, and there would be nothing to astonish him if he followed the same track to-day. We step straight from the new town into the old country. An occasional rumble on the left tells us that a railway-line is near, but it runs unseen in the hollow, and we look across it to the trees of Wilton Park. Our path runs straight, sometimes through open fields, sometimes through woods of oaks and beeches, with pigeons cooing in the branches and yellow ragwort and purple willow-herb ramping in every clearing, or, again, through a low-growing covert where silver birches rise above the gorse. In all the two miles and a quarter from Maltmans Green to the Jordans enclave we pass but one house, a picturesque old keeper's cottage on the outskirts of Layters Green, standing beneath graceful poplars on the only lane we have to cross.

A mile and a half from Layters Green we enter Welders Lane, at the point where it descends the short steep hill to the road junction by Jordans Meeting-house; but, if we cross the lane and pursue the bridle-path opposite as far as the road from Chalfont St. Giles, we shall start with the house that comes first in the story. The little eminence that rises to separate the two converging roads gives us an extensive view of the surrounding country, with the heights of Coleshill in front of us and the hills bordering the Misbourne valley to the right; and as we descend the further slope we have on our left an orchard leading

Charles R. Bassent 1875

OLD JORDANS FARM

to the pleasant group of buildings shown in Mr. Bathurst's drawing. This is Old Jordans Farm, which was purchased by the Society of Friends in 1911 and converted into the Jordans Hostel. The main portion is typically Georgian, and there is Jacobean work within. The old stables and outbuildings have been altered to serve the purpose of refectory and dormitories, but all the new construction made necessary by the change from farm to hostel is perfectly in keeping with the earlier portion. In the peaceful quadrangle formed by these outbuildings a little sunk garden has been made with a sundial in the centre. On the south side, with its end abutting on the road, a picturesque barn of weathered oak has been turned into a large room for meetings and conferences by the addition of floor and windows. This barn is of particular interest owing to the tradition that it was built of timbers from the " Mayflower," which carried the Pilgrim Fathers overseas. This tradition has been examined in detail by Professor Rendel Harris in *The Finding of the Mayflower*, published at the time of the tercentenary of the voyage. There is no doubt that the timber came from some ship of much the same size that sailed the seas at much the same time. It is known that the " Mayflower " was broken up on the Thames in 1624 and the year would agree roughly with the probable date of erection; moreover, an old door in the house has a carved panel representing something like a mayflower which may have decorated the same vessel. Again, Bradford's *Journal* of the voyage of the " Mayflower " states that a beam was broken and mended with a clamp from a printing-press: a broken beam mended with a piece of iron may be seen in the barn, and it bears the initials HA, said to be the mark of Harwich, where the " Mayflower " was registered. But it is curious that none of these early Quakers, who were keenly interested in America, ever mentioned the fact in their voluminous writings.

At the time when Quakerism first entered the Chalfont country—in the days of the Commonwealth—Old Jordans Farm was occupied by William Russell, who joined the new sect and endured much persecution. In the " Return of Conventicles " made in 1669 his house in Giles Chalfont is mentioned as a place where sixty or seventy persons of " inconsiderable qualitie " met for worship, with Isaac Penington as their " head or teacher." Here they continued to gather till the Meeting-house was built in 1688 in the hollow below, probably using the old Jacobean kitchen which still remains. Thomas Ellwood records that he was present when two raids were made upon the meetings by informers, and paints the characters of these instruments of the law in lurid colours. The chief informer was Poulter, son of a Salisbury butcher, who had long " been there branded for a Fellow egregiously wicked and debauched." Since two witnesses were required to prove " illegal assembly," Poulter found a colleague in Ralph Lacy of Risborough, who had recently been " released out of Aylesbury Jail, where he very narrowly escaped the Gallows for having stolen a Cow "; while a third, a " broken ironmonger " of High Wycombe called Aris, who had contemplated becoming a highwayman, afterwards took the place of Poulter, who had become too well known for his own safety. The Minutes of the Jordans Meeting, quoted by Mr. Summers, give a vivid account of the first raid in July 1670. Penn's friend, the saintly George Whitehead, happened to be present. The informers had obtained a warrant and took the parish constable with them. Poulter at first remained in the background, and sent Ralph Lacy with Dell, a local youth who had been bribed to identify the worshippers, into the meeting.

" Upon the 24th of the fifth month [July], 1670, some of the people of God (whom the world called Quakers) were peaceably met together at the house of William Russell at Jordans, in the parish of Giles Chalfont, to wait upon and worship the Lord God of Heaven, in truth and sincerity, according to the requirements of his good Spirit and as the Holy Scriptures direct, in which religious exercise, as we were sitting together, attentively giving heed unto what the Lord by ye mouth of one of his servants did at that time minister unto us; Henry Reading, one of ye constables of ye said parish . . . came

in amongst us, attended by one Ralph Lacy and John
Dell, in yᵉ quality of informers, and one Richard Dunton
as assistant, and showing us a warrant under yᵉ hand and
seal of Edward Baldwin, of Wilson's Green, in the parish
of Beaconsfield, a Commissioner of the Peace for the said
county, he commanded us forthwith to go before him.
But we who came not together in man's wil, but according to the requirings of yᵉ Lord, could not consent to
break up our meeting in the wil, or by the command of
men. We, therefore, continuing thus waiting upon the
Lord, his servant G.W. after some time kneeled down to
prayer, which, when Lacy, the informer, perceived, he
forthwith stept aside, and, with a whistle called in another
fellow, tenfold more a child of the devil than himself.
This was Poulter, who, like a savage brute, with hideous
noise, rushing in amongst us, laid hold on G.W. while in
prayer, and in an outrageous manner dragged him along
yᵉ floor, not without great danger of hurt, had not the
Lord prevented him. A fitter instrument than this fellow
Satan could scarce have found; for his rage and enmity,
fury and madness, which appeared in his face, words and
actions, rendered him more a monster than a man. . . ."

The incident ended in the usual way with the infliction
of heavy fines on the worshippers—William Russell £20
and the others smaller sums; but when the informers made
a second raid they met their match. This time Lacy and
Aris were the interrupters, with Dell again accompanying
them, and, seeing much the same congregation in the
room, swore to the presence of the same people who had
been fined before. On their list was Thomas Zachary, a
well-known London doctor who had a house at Beaconsfield; he had been present at the first meeting but was in
London at the time of the second raid. Fined in his absence, Zachary appealed and proved his alibi on the evidence of London friends too eminent for the local
justices to disregard them. Ellwood then took up the
prosecution of the informers for perjury, and, in spite
of all obstacles placed in his way, won his case at Quarter
Sessions. The prisoners absconded. Aris fled the country:

" the other (Lacy) lurked privily for a while in Woods and By-places, till Hunger and Want forced him out." On Zachary's intercession, Ellwood agreed to let the warrant for his arrest remain in abeyance. " Thus," writes Ellwood, " began and thus ended the informing Trade in these parts of the County of *Bucks*; the ill Success that these first Informers found, discouraged all others, how vile soever, from attempting the like Enterprize there ever after. . . ."

George Fox, the founder of the Society of Friends, visited Jordans Farm in 1673 and again in 1677 for important meetings; and in 1676 old William Russell, " near eighty and almost blind," suffered his last term of imprisonment, though he continued to be fined for non-payment of tithes. Already in 1671 William Russell and another had sold part of the land called Well Close Hedgerow on trust to Thomas Ellwood, Thomas Zachary and four other Quakers, acting for the Meeting, to form a Quaker burial-ground. It is noteworthy that the principal vendor and all the purchasers had been in gaol. Here burials began at once: William Russell's daughter was among the first, and Isaac Penington and his wife Mary, old William Russell himself, and three children of William and Guli Penn, who died at Rickmansworth, were all laid to rest in this little graveyard while Jordans Farm was still the meeting-house. In June 1788 came the next advance: William Russell the younger sold to Isaac Penington's son John " a plot of ground called Well Close Hedgerow, together with the Dell of Wood therein, containing 1 acre. Also the corner of a close of land called Coarse Hurdles, containing 1 acre 3 roods." While the throne of James II was tottering, the Jordans Meeting-house was erected without the slightest interruption; it was finished before William of Orange landed at Torbay on November 5, and young Penington, the nominal purchaser, formally handed over the completed building to trustees on behalf of the Society. William Penn is said to have been a generous subscriber towards the expense.

Descending the road from Old Jordans Farm we come at once to the little graveyard, a narrow croft with a few

unornamented headstones beneath the shadow of surrounding limes, running from the orchard of the farm
to the corner in the valley bottom, where the road from
Chalfont St. Giles meets Welders Lane.   Behind it, in
another little plot, separated from it by a wooden paling,
stands the simple red-brick Meeting-house with its adjoining cottage.   At the back the ground rises steeply from
a dell, formed long ago by excavations for chalk or gravel,
and this escarpment with its crown of beech-trees, and
the limes and chestnuts of Stone Dean across the road,
unite to form a screen behind the little building where
William Penn worshipped and the narrow paddock where
he was brought to rest worn out by a life of labour for
good in two continents.

The little group of headstones erected in memory of
the Penns, Penington, Ellwoods and a few other forefathers of the Quaker faith are all of recent date, and
give no idea of the great number buried in this little
plot.   The Devonshire House register gives the names of
134 Quakers buried at Jordans between 1671 and 1724,
and for many years no mark distinguished their several
graves.   But a plan was kept, and a copy was preserved
by the Butterfield family of Stone Dean.   The present
stones roughly mark the resting-places of those whose
names they bear; that of William Penn between those of
his two wives is probably the most correct, for the spot
was indicated by Prince Butterfield, who saw the leaden
coffin of the Quaker statesman when his second wife was
buried in 1726, and lived till the early years of the nine-
teenth century.   The Meeting-house itself has been so
often described by pen and picture that there is little left
to say.   But it serves to prove how pleasant a simple,
unornamented building can look if it is built of good
material and in good proportions.   Restfulness is its prevailing note.   The interior, with its plain whitewashed
walls and wooden forms, is equally unassuming.   The most
curious feature is the gallery, which can be shut off from
the large room by a wooden shutter.   A common explanation—that this was where the Quakers hid when enemies
came—is obviously proved false by the testimony of

honest Thomas Ellwood.   Not only in the raids at Old
Jordans, but in others at Hedgerley Dean and Wooburn,
there was no attempt to run away; and, when the troop
of yeomanry came to Chalfont Grange, it was a non-
Quaker visitor who ran out and hid in the garden, and
Ellwood makes a good story of his abject contrition afterwards.   The Quakers just sat still.   It is probable that the
room formed by the closed gallery was occupied by the
Women's Meeting, which was then held separately from
the Men's; and it is now used as an extra bedroom for the
caretaker's cottage.

Two other neighbouring houses play their part in the
history of Jordans.   Welders Lane, coming from Chalfont
St. Peters, receives on its right the road from Chalfont
St. Giles at the corner of Jordans burial-place.   A few
yards further on a road runs up the valley, on the right
again, to Seer Green and so forward to Penn or Coleshill; and Welders Lane continues up the opposite slope to
curve round Wilton Park to Beaconsfield.   Throughout
the valley Welders Lane is bordered on the left by the
grounds of Stone Dean; and in the angle between the
road to Chalfont St. Giles and that to Seer Green the picturesque Dean Farm sits among its gabled barns and
rickyards.   Both of these houses for many years offered
hospitality to those who came from distant places to visit
Jordans.   Of their activities we get our best account in
the record left by Rebekah Butterfield, who lived first
at Stone Dean and afterwards at Dean Farm.   Her diary,
preserved in the library of the Friends' Meeting-house
opposite Euston Station in London, is a mine of information on the early days of Chiltern Quakerism.   The first
portion of it was evidently copied from an earlier record
written by one " A. L.," who may be identified as Alice
Lovelace, who lived with her husband Joseph at Dean
Farm.   Rebekah Butterfield's own account only ceases
shortly before her death in 1774, and is then continued
by her son, Prince Butterfield.

At the very beginning comes a note that " This house
called Stone Dean was built by My Uncle Peter Prince "
in 1691.   Prince was a " citizen and tallow-chandler " of

Handley & Brathwaite 428

STONE DEAN.

Hammersmith, and in 1685 had married Mary Odingsells of Chalfont St. Peter at Old Jordans. He built his country home right in the bottom of the little valley, and its grounds, extending up the slopes on either side—limes and spreading chestnuts about the house and beechwoods above—might have been specially designed to preserve for Jordans Meeting-house its Quaker-like seclusion. The white front of the house, facing the lane, is obviously a later addition, but the square brick building behind, with the curious little belfry on its tiled roof, must be substantially the home that sheltered many an early pilgrim to the shrine of William Penn. The little lattice window shown on the left of Mr. Bathurst's picture is said by tradition to light the room where Penn himself was left to meditate during his visits. This historic chamber lies apart from the main house, across an open passage and up steep steps. It still has the old roof beams, and the windows also probably date from the time of William Penn.

Merely to turn the leaves of Rebekah's diary, noting the firm clear handwriting gradually weaken as old age crept on, seems to bring one nearer to her times and into closer touch with the friends she met and fed at her own table. In her industrious pages, amid many details of her family and her visitors, we can note landmarks in the Quakers' progress from outlawry and persecution into calmer waters. Her uncle died in September 1694.

"My dear Uncle Peter Prince departed this Life at his own house called Stone Dean & was Buried at Jordans. William Penn & Robert Barrow & several other Publick Friends & also a great number of Friends and others."

In 1707 her own wedding is recorded: "George Bowles, John Field and John Kent was at ye marriage of Abraham Butterfield to Rebekah Webb, one of Peter Prince's nieces, at Jordans." Her aunt married again and again became a widow, and the Butterfields came from Coleshill to join her at Stone Dean. Meanwhile, one by one, the earliest members of the Meeting were passing away: the burials

3

of Gulielma Penn, of the Peningtons, of the Ellwoods are recorded in turn: and then, in 1718—

"Our Friend William Penn Departed at Rushcom in Berkshire in ye 74th year of his Age and was Buried att Jordans ye 5th of ye 6th mo. ye 3rd day of ye week. There was 20 or 30 Publick Friends and a Vast Number of friends & others. He was often at Jordans meeting in his Life time and often lodged at Stone Dean."

When Abraham Butterfield died in 1756 he must have been one of the last of the local yeomen who, under the leadership of the courtly Penn and the mystic Penington, had formed the rank and file in the Quaker vanguard. From 1730 onwards there are frequent entries of visitors from distant parts. They came from Scotland, Ireland, Holland and nearly every English county; and in 1732 "Ann Robarts of Gwineth or Northwales in America & Mary Pennel living near Concord in Chester County in Pensilvania" came to Jordans Meeting and spent two nights at Stone Dean. Two Pennsylvanians attended the funeral of Margaret Freame, the last to survive of William Penn's children, and many others followed. Americans were usually entertained by the Butterfields, for Rebekah's sister had settled with her husband in Maryland. The altered position of Quakers is indicated by an entry under the year 1729 when " the Dutchess of Portland " came over from Bulstrode to attend a funeral; and in 1733, when John Langthorn married Sarah Lane, " ye Duke of Portland and ye Lady Anne his sister was at Jordans Meett: at ye marriage and set their hands to ye Certificate." The little stable beneath the Meeting-house that had sufficed to shelter the riding-horses of the early worshippers soon was unable to contain the equipages of these later days, when one funeral was attended by " 8 coches, 3 lose horses and a carriage beside."

But conditions were changing. The growth of big towns was attended by a decrease of the rural population: Jordans was found a less convenient centre than High Wycombe, Amersham or Chesham and its regular services were discontinued in 1799. The graveyard was constantly used for burials for another thirty years, many wealthy Quaker families in London and other towns bringing their dead to rest in its historic soil. The grave of William Penn brought a continuous train of pilgrims. But it was only in 1910, when the tide of population began to surge back again from the towns, that regular Sunday services were re-established in the little Meeting-house. Old Jordans Farm was, as we have seen, purchased a year later for a Hostel, and throughout the Great War became the busy training centre of the Friends' Ambulance Unit. In 1918 another important step was taken in the preservation of Jordans. The Dean Farm estate came into the market, and the gabled homestead and 100 acres of land were purchased by members of the Society of Friends in order to save from speculative builders the fields immediately facing the Meeting-house. Since houses were needed in the district, a part of the ground lying out of sight over the ridge was laid out as the site of a new village, and conveyed, upon certain conditions, to a registered society called Jordans Village, Ltd. Here a not unpleasing group of brick cottages has been built; each resident has a share in the society, and the village is controlled, in accordance with the articles of association, by an elected committee, with one outside member appointed by the Society of Friends. When Stone Dean a few years later passed again into the possession of a Friend, the peacefulness of the little Jordans hollow appeared to be fully safeguarded. Then the local District Council tried its hand at town-planning, and the fruits of all this loving labour are again in jeopardy.

As we leave the gateway of Stone Dean and follow the road that runs westward up the valley to Seer Green village, we pass Dean Farm on the right, and, turning back, take our last look at Jordans. The Meeting-house and the three houses associated with it lie close together within a ring fence, occupying in all an infinitesimal space upon the map. The valley is narrow, and a width of less than 800 yards would afford complete protection to the whole. Yet right through the middle, breaking up the grounds of Stone Dean and cutting it off from the Meeting-house, it is proposed to drive a great main road for motor traffic. The plan has not unnaturally met with strenuous opposition and an inquiry has been held. The result is still in doubt: but what other nation, one wonders, if it possessed an inheritance so unique as Jordans, would contemplate the destruction of its whole character in order that the motorist might start two minutes later upon his journey?

The station of Seer Green Halt is beset by advertisements of speculators in land: a vast signboard on the skyline would seem to defeat its own avowed object of tempting passers-by to make a rural home beneath it. But here the devastated area is of small extent. We leave it behind us as we climb the hill to Seer Green, while beyond the railway lie woodland glades of uncommon beauty where the Beaconsfield golfers take their pleasure. Seer Green itself is still a little country village, perched on a spur, with space for orchards about the cottages and rickyards bordering the village street. A straight footpath, running across open fields to the right, would bring us out upon the road again at Butler's Cross, and so forward to Chalfont St. Giles within a three-mile walk; but having arrived thus far, and become steeped in Quaker traditions, let those of us who will push on to Hunger Hill, where Thomas Ellwood lived and died, and then descend from Coleshill by an excellent footpath to the same village.

The little street of Seer Green is divided by a sharp peninsula on which stands the church, but it matters not which way we choose. If we go to the right past the " Cricketers' Arms " we turn to the left at Rawlings Farm a mile further on; and if we choose the left-hand road we take the next turn to the right. Both bring us to the same spot where a cart-track enters the southernmost angle of Hodgemoor Wood. Inside it we take a footpath to the left, and, traversing a mile of varied woodland, descend steeply through beeches to the Beaconsfield-Amersham road. From the corner by the Magpies Inn a lane runs up to the southern spur of Coleshill, and Ellwood's Hunger

Hill, now called Ongar Hill, lies half-way up the slope. He himself described the place in verse for the benefit of an expected visitor:

> " Two miles from Beaconsfield, upon the road
>   To Amersham, just where the way grows broad,
>   A little spot there is called Larkin's Green,
>   Where on a bank some fruit trees may be seen ;
>   In midst of which, on the sinister hand,
>   A little cottage covertly doth stand.
>   ' Soho ! ' the people out and then inquire
>   For Hunger Hill ; it lies a little higher.
>   But if the people should from home be gone,
>   Ride up the bank some twenty paces on,
>   And at the orchard's end thou may'st perceive
>   Two gates together hung.   The nearest leave,
>   The farthest take, and straight the hill ascend,
>   That path leads to the house where dwells thy friend."

The little cottage still stands " covertly " behind the " Magpies," but Ellwood's farm-house, decayed beyond repair, was rebuilt in recent years. Yet it is good to see his surroundings still unchanged: as his old friend George Bowles testified at his death, " He hath left a sweet Savour behind him." " His heart and House," runs another testimony, " was open to his Friends, and the Monthly Meeting was kept there more than Forty Years and remains there to this day."   The position of the farm had a certain convenience in Ellwood's day, for it was included with Coleshill in a little Hertfordshire island lying in the midst of Buckinghamshire.   No warrant issued by Buckinghamshire magistrates had power within it, and the minions of the law who persecuted Quakers at Jordans or Chalfont Grange had no such licence here.   The Hertfordshire authorities only sent an expeditionary force on rare occasions when there was a sufficient number of substantial Quakers in residence to make it worth their while, and then were unable to touch those who had stepped over the Buckinghamshire border to attend the Meeting.

We ascend the steep slope to the windmill on Coleshill Common because Coleshill is a pleasant place in itself and it also enjoys a notable prospect. The ground falls away on every side, and the heights of Penn stand out across the valley to the west; both rise like bastions from the Beaconsfield plateau and form a sharp line of demarcation between the Upper Chilterns and the lower slopes. Of Beaconsfield we see little save the old church tower, with red splashes of its new town peeping not unpleasantly among the trees. Behind, Windsor Castle and the forest ridges. Coleshill village follows the L-shaped contours of its hill. Its common runs irregularly down the side and there are many interesting old houses. A very picturesque cottage on the road to Winchmore Hill might be almost any age, certainly no younger than the sixteenth century. I spoke of it to a native. " Yes," he said, " it's very old: it must have been built quite a hundred years ago." Coleshill, indeed, deserves a longer visit, but we take a footpath to the right opposite the church and descend to the Amersham road. To our left, at the head of the valley, Coleshill House shines white among its trees. Here was born Edmund Waller, the poet; but the present house is mostly of later date and we shall meet him again at Beaconsfield. Across the road the course of our path becomes obscure; but a rudimentary style will be found a few yards to the right of our point of entry, and the path becomes clear again where it skirts the little cottage at the back of Brentford Grange. Thenceforward our route lies clear through unbroken country. There is nothing striking about it, nothing to cause surprise. We follow a hedge where white beam turns to silver in the wind; we dive into a lane and out again and catch the scent of honeysuckle as we pass; we cross a red-brown field lately turned by the plough. Beechwoods are never far away, and every hollow brings fresh views of the valley on the left. All the way there is " nothing to write home about," as the saying goes; but the sense of fresh air and restfulness will make the walk worth while to every lover of the English countryside. We ascend a long pasture where sheep browse beneath the hawthorns, and, from the final ridge near Hill Farm, look down upon the Chalfonts, with the Chiltern foothills descending to the plain at Denham and at Fulmer, and the Surrey downs closing the view

between. Close below us are the red roofs of Bottrells
Farm, where Ellwood found lodgings for Mary Penington
and her children, and we pass beneath it as we follow a
lane to Chalfont St. Giles.

Chalfont St. Giles is shaped like a Y with the broad
down-stroke resting on the main road that runs up the
valley to Amersham. The passing motorist should not
be deterred by the shouting advertisements that defile
every vacant space at the cross-roads, for the village, once
you are within it, still upholds its reputation as the prettiest village in the district. Nor has it the self-conscious-
ness that mars so many fashionable beauty-spots. It is
still just a simple village of old houses, with a pond in
the centre placed just right to reflect the church tower
behind. Mr. Bathurst has caught it as the evening
shadows fall across the street. Through the old timbered
house beyond the pool we gain access to the church, which
looks over open fields to the south. The walls within
are covered with fragments of fourteenth-century paint-
ings; many of the subjects are difficult to identify, but
Salome turning a somersault, as mediæval painters so frequently portray her, is conspicuous among them. The
most prominent monuments are to successive owners of
The Vache. Bishop Hare rests from his campaigns in the
south aisle, and the many dignities of Admiral Sir Hugh
Palliser are set out on a spacious tablet opposite. In the
chancel is an interesting altar tomb portraying Thomas
Fleetwood, the Master of the Mint, with his two wives
and eighteen children. The chancel window is said to
have been damaged by Cromwell's cannon firing in the
Meads. Cromwell himself was entertained by the Rat-
cliffes at The Stone, which stands at the corner of the
main road; the present house is of later date and it is
possible that it was Stone Farm behind, a low timbered
house beside the Misbourne, that sheltered the Lord
Protector.

Outside the church the street divides. By the arm on
the right we arrived, and we follow the other to visit
Milton's Cottage, the show-place of the village. We find
it on our left where the row of houses ends, with a little

garden beside it. Early visitors speak of a porch which has disappeared; but the house was purchased by subscription in 1887 and is now safe as a well-kept museum. Of John Milton's visit in 1665 we get the best account from Thomas Ellwood: let him tell his own story.

" Some little time before I went to *Aylesbury* Prison, I was desired by my *quondam* Master *Milton,* to take an House for him in the Neighbourhood where I dwelt, that he might go out of the City, for the Safety of himself and his Family, the Pestilence then growing hot in *London.* I took a pretty Box for him in Giles-Chalfont, a Mile from me, of which I gave him Notice, and intended to have waited on him, and seen him well settled in it, but was prevented by that Imprisonment.

" But now being released and returned home, I soon made a Visit to him, to welcome him into the County.

" After some common Discourses had passed between us, he called for a *Manuscript* of his; which being brought he delivered to me, bidding me take it home with me, and read it at my Leisure; and when I had so done, return it to him with my Judgment thereupon.

" When I came home, and had set myself to read it, I found it was that excellent Poem which he entituled PARADISE LOST. After I had, with the best Attention, read it through, I made him another Visit, and returned him his Book, with due Acknowledgement of the Favour he had done me in communicating it to me. He asked me, *How I liked it, and what I thought of it?* which I modestly but freely told him; and after some further Discourse about it, I pleasantly said to him, Thou hast said much here about *Paradise lost*; but what hast thou to say of *Paradise found?* He made me no Answer, but sate some Time in a Muse; then brake off that Discourse, and fell upon another Subject.

After the Sickness was over, and the City well cleansed and become safely habitable again, he returned thither. And when afterwards I went to wait on him there (which I seldom failed to do) he showed me his second Poem, called PARADISE REGAINED; and in a pleasant Tone said to me, *This is owing to you; for you put it into my Head by the Question you put to me at* Chalfont; *which before I had not thought of.*"

That is all we know about Milton's sojourn here. The story that Judge Jeffreys came over to insult him seems as baseless as the prettier tale that Guli Springett came down from Bottrells Farm to play the lute and sing to him. But the quiet little cottage where the blind poet wrote the last lines of *Paradise Lost* is a fitting place to end a peaceful day that began with Jordans.

CHAPTER IV

AMONG GREAT HOUSES

ON Gerrards Cross Common the main road to Oxford is crossed by another running to Stoke Poges and Slough. This latter road and the whole country to the east of it have been amazingly transformed in recent times. A few years before the War a walker could step out of Uxbridge, and wandering towards Beaconsfield by almost any route lose himself at once in a wild country of woods and commons. To-day only patches of country remain in a sea of new settlements, and the movement yet continues. Many of these patches are still beautiful. Denham, the swan-song of the Misbourne valley, retains its quiet, well-bred air in its sheltered by-pass, and in footpaths through a wood or across a common we may for a moment forget that any changes have occurred. But he who seeks a thoroughly country walk must pick his way with care. There is one good avenue still remaining from Uxbridge to the Penn Country. Once we have run the gauntlet of New Denham and its wireless station, we can turn up the lane by Hillbrook Place and, following the Alder Bourne upwards, find the old beauty of Fulmer quite untarnished. Thence we have a smooth passage by the wide expanse of Stoke Common to Hollybush Corner or Hedgerley. But even here we can never diverge far from the strait path without losing the country feeling. From the Thames valley on the south there is the same difficulty of approach. Burnham, Stoke and Farnham began to assume a " residential " air with the coming of the Great Western Railway, and, now that a great manufacturing centre is springing up all along the northern side of the line from Slough to Burnham Beeches Station, incidentally eating up some of the richest cornlands in England, the invasion of bricks and mortar is daily accelerating its pace.

Yet west of this cross-road from Gerrards Cross to Slough we can still find England as it was. We can cross the wide ridge from side to side, from Gerrards Cross Common to the Thames, and walk in real country all the way. It is not that the wave of new population has suddenly stopped. Gerrards Cross has more than quadrupled its inhabitants in twenty years. Beaconsfield has doubled its houses, and, on the western side, the separate little villages that used to stud the valley from Cookham to High Wycombe will soon be an almost continuous town. But the population is more wisely placed: grouped together to share the benefits of civilization, and leaving wide stretches of healthful country between which all may enjoy. Regional planning is no new invention: it has been practised, perhaps unconsciously, by great landowners for many a generation. We step straight into open country to-day from Gerrards Cross, as we might from Beaconsfield or Wooburn or Bourne End, because we are going to walk among great houses. " Let us now praise famous men. . . . Rich men, furnished with ability, living peaceably in their own habitations."

The old brick wall of Bulstrode Park borders the Oxford Road and one of its great gates stands in the corner of Gerrards Cross Common. At the little keeper's cottage, a hundred yards along the road towards Beaconsfield, the footpath begins which takes us for the first mile of our journey through the manifold beauties of Bulstrode. From the traffic of the high road we pass into another world. Arthur Young, who had visited parks innumerable, placed it among the finest he remembered, and grew lyrical about its " elegant varieties . . . its perpetual swells and slopes set off by scattered plantations, disposed in the justest taste." There is not one level acre in all its eight hundred; its seclusion to north and east and south is preserved by its own wooded hills, and to the south-west, at the end of the long sloping valley that our footpath follows, the view is bounded by the more distant trees of Hedgerley Park.

The mansion rises on the hill to our right and looks over the woods to Windsor and the Surrey downs beyond; but the present house was only completed in 1866, while the park has endured for a thousand years, preserved by one owner after another from love of its beauty. For traces of its early history we must look to our left. The long sloping ridge that bounds our valley is broken at one point, and through the gap we see the only abrupt ascent in the park. The difficulty of the climb possibly owes something to human effort, for on the top lies an extensive camp surrounded by earth-works. This camp played a prominent part in the early history of the place, if we may believe the long-established traditions of the Bulstrode family, as related to the herald, Sir Bernard Burke.[1] The story goes that the park was already existing before the Conquest and was given by William the Norman to one of his followers. But one Shobington, the Saxon owner, was in no mood to be dispossessed of so fair a place without a struggle. Having notice of the imminent loss of his inheritance, he armed his retainers and called to his aid his neighbours, Pen of Pen and Hampden of Hampden. In this camp they awaited the coming of the Norman lord with his thousand soldiers. The Normans camped in the valley below, and in the night Shobington and his allies mounted on bulls and charged them, killing many and driving the rest into terror-stricken flight. King William, hearing of this daring feat, gave Shobington a safe conduct to come to Court, and there Shobington went, riding on his bull with his seven sons behind him. As a result of this interview, Shobington became William's loyal vassal, was reinstated in his ancestral lands, and bore thenceforth the name of Shobington Bulstrode. It is possible that the evidence of his story might not satisfy professed historians, but those who like to believe it can point to the camp which lies just where the Bulstrode archives place it, and can vow that this valley bottom where we walk, amid acres of open park, is a place where the stoutest soldier well might quail before a company of bulls charging headlong down the grassy slope.

[1] *Vicissitudes of Families*, by Sir Bernard Burke, Vol. II.

The mediæval history of Bulstrode is shadowy: Templars and Hospitallers, the nuns of Burnham and the canons of Bisham, all appear at one time or another as owning a part or the whole of the manor. But when bluff King Henry swept away the religious houses, the Bulstrodes emerge again recovered from their bull-fight, and with their descendants, the Whitelockes, remained as owners of Bulstrode for another century. Bulstrode Whitelocke, the Lord Keeper of the Commonwealth and author of *Memorials* of his age, inherited it as son of Sir James Whitelocke and Elizabeth Bulstrode. He is said to have let it for a time to Praise-God Barebones, the zealous Puritan who gave his name to the " Barebones " Parliament. He possessed other residences near Henley, suffered losses in the Civil War, and had many children; and Bulstrode soon passed out of the hands of the alleged descendants of Shobington the Saxon.

The position of the earliest house is unknown, but a new mansion was certainly built on the site occupied by the present one by the notorious Judge Jeffreys. He had purchased the property before 1681, for in that year he was created a baronet as Sir George Jeffreys of Bulstrode; but his new house was not completed till 1686. We know that it was built of red brick because his neighbours, remembering the Bloody Assizes, asserted that it was stained with blood. Here Jeffreys entertained King James II and Queen Mary of Modena, but soon after his downfall and death the place was sold by his son-in-law. Whitelocke the Roundhead and Jeffreys the Jacobite were followed by William Bentinck, Earl of Portland, the staunch supporter and friend of William of Orange, who spent his days of retirement amid these hills and valleys. The Earl's grandson, the second Duke of Portland, made Bulstrode his favourite residence, and had the distinction of being robbed by the highwayman, Dick Turpin, in his own park. He married Lady Margaret Harley, granddaughter and heiress of the Duke of Newcastle, who brought Welbeck Abbey and other property to swell the Bentinck estates. Celebrated in her childhood as " my noble, lovely, little Peggy " by the poet Prior, she lived to become a very distinguished hostess at Bulstrode and a noted patron of literature and the arts. In their day the house was greatly altered. Horace Walpole came over several times from Chalfont Park, but it failed to please his Gothic taste. He found it " Dutch and trist . . . a melancholy monument of Dutch magnificence," and even when the hospitable Duchess made him a gift of surplus pictures he accepts them with a sneer. But everybody else seems to have admired it, and the raptures of the Bluestocking leaders, Mrs. Montague and Mrs. Delany, who were the Duchess's lifelong friends, more than made up for Walpole's cynical comments. " We arrived on Sunday," wrote Mrs. Montague on her first visit, when she was still Elizabeth Robinson, " at the most charming place I ever saw; a very magnificent house, fine gardens, and a beautiful park." There were aviaries of strange birds, beds of curious flowers, and galleries full of pictures; the famous Portland Vase stood among lesser treasures in the drawing-room; and any house-party might have formed a ministry of all the talents.

With the third Duke, Lord-Lieutenant of Ireland and twice Prime Minister, the atmosphere of Bulstrode became more strictly political. Lord Malmesbury records many discussions within its walls. Burke brought over friends from Beaconsfield; another Prime Minister, Lord Grenville, was living at Dropmore, and this little corner of Buckinghamshire saw a constant coming and going of statesmen of all parties. This Duke pulled down a great part of the house, intending to rebuild it, but died before the work was put in hand. His son sold it to the Duke of Somerset, and his descendant Sir John Ramsden is the present owner.

We leave the park by the south gate and follow the lane to the right which soon divides. We take the footpath that bisects the angle and follow it through the fields down a peaceful valley which brings us to the village of Hedgerley. The church stands high upon a hill to our right. From it we look down upon a little hamlet which no modern changes have invaded. From the half-timbered cottage on the right, with projecting upper story, down

CLIVEDEN.

to the cross-roads at the other end where a Georgian house of mellow brick stands above the pond, the whole place might have stepped out of another century. The little inn at the corner is quaintly named " The Brick Mould," and blessed be the mould that gave the texture to its bricks. The little row of cottages among which it stands has no ornament save its good proportions; but the soft surface of the bricks, toned with age, gives to the group a charm never attainable with the hard shiny bricks so often used by modern builders.

Turning the corner to the right past the little village hall we soon come to Pennlands Farm, where we can see the craft of brickmaking in progress. It is just the kind of place where good bricks should be made—the bricks stacked in well-thatched shelters, willows growing in the dark-red excavations and a wide view of woods and valleys as we look back upon the way we have come. From the brickyard we pass through a gate to the main road from Slough to Beaconsfield. Beaconsfield lies two miles to the north, half a mile to the south the houses of Farnham Common begin; here the open country has been preserved, and the only house in sight is a wayside inn. We are still among great estates. We take a gate opposite and enter the property of Lord Burnham. A broad track runs through a low-growing copse where sapling birches rise from beds of heather and bracken, and Egypt woods run along the high ground on the left. Bearing to the right all the way, we eventually come out at Abbey Park Farm and follow the road forward which brings us quickly to Littleworth Common.

We have already passed upon our left a lane running through woods to Burnham Beeches, the southern extremity of a great forest running continuously from Egypt Wood through a corner of which we skirted. There are still some glorious trees among the Beeches and pleasant walks among their four hundred acres; but, since their purchase by the Corporation of London in 1879, orderly drives have been driven through them and their wilderness has been tamed. They remain a valuable open space and give pleasure to thousands of London picnickers. But there are two villages, to the east and to the west, which may claim to be included in the Penn Country through their connection with sons of William Penn. At Hitcham, two miles to the south-west, lived John Penn, eldest son of William by his second wife, who succeeded his father as proprietor of Pennsylvania; and in that peaceful spot he died in 1746. Thomas Penn, his brother and successor, lived at Stoke Poges, half a mile to the east, having purchased the old Manor House in Stoke Park, the history of which is sung by Gray in *The Long Story*. He married, curiously enough, Lady Juliana Fermor, granddaughter of Judge Jeffreys of Bulstrode. Their son, John Penn, rich with the purchase money of Pennsylvania, had an entirely new house erected, built for him by Wyatt from designs by Nasmyth; and it was he who raised on a pillar in the park the statue of that great lawyer Sir Edward Coke, a former owner of the Manor House, and placed by the pathway in the country churchyard the cenotaph in memory of Thomas Gray which looks so out of place to modern eyes. Both these villages retain much of their former beauty. At Hitcham still blooms the walled Elizabethan garden, where Sir William Clarke, Queen Elizabeth's physician, received his sovereign with a pomp that seemed presumptuous to jealous eyes. At Stoke Poges the grey church still lifts " its ivy-mantled tower " among the " rugged elms," much as the poet saw it when he began to write his *Elegy*. Golf links and a country club still contrive to keep an open space about this haunt of literary pilgrims. But both villages are something of oases in an advancing desert of new houses, and are best visited by car.

We turn back to Littleworth Common and, at its further edge, come to the hospitable gates of Dropmore. Twice a week the gardens may be seen, and at any time a well-behaved visitor may walk along the carriage-drives and admire the wonderful collection of exotic trees. The park, which extends to some 600 acres, was rough open country, like Littleworth Common, till 1792, when Lord Grenville, cousin of the younger Pitt, purchased it and made his home there. He was a younger son of

George Grenville, who, as Chancellor of the Exchequer, had forwarded the passing of the American Stamp Act and so lit the train of powder that led to the outburst of the War of Independence. Lord Grenville himself was also a prominent politician and was Prime Minister of the Coalition Government that passed the Act of 1807 for the abolition of the slave trade. After his purchase of the Dropmore property, its improvement occupied all his leisure. If the soil was poor, tons of earth were carted from other places. To his wife he left the garden, but trees were his never-failing delight. He died here in 1834, and the property passed to the descendants of his sister, Lady Fortescue, who still possess it.

Our road lies westward, and the drive through Dropmore is our nearest way. The saplings Lord Grenville planted tower above us on either side, with rhododendrons underneath. Near the house the ground is more open, with giant deodars here and there and a group of spreading cedars of Lebanon to frame the view. Pines, Wellingtonias and monkey-puzzles all do credit to his lordship's planting. If it be Monday or Saturday we can visit the trim Italian garden and descend through a ramping wilderness of flowers to the lake below. But on any day we can continue our course round the park amid an infinite variety of trees, all superbly grown. Golden pheasants, scuttling into shrubberies, provide a bright splash of colour, but those undesirable aliens, the grey squirrels, are far too numerous. The gate that leads to Hedsor we passed near the house; the next brings us out a little short of the three cross-roads christened Nobleman's Corner, as leading to Hedsor, Dropmore and Cliveden. Here our walk is practically accomplished. We set out to walk across this ridge to the river through open country all the way, and only a narrow strip of Cliveden divides us from the steep bank descending to the Thames.

The only good view of Cliveden from a public place is from the river-side, where Mr. Bathurst has made his drawing; and the woods descending from its slopes, adjoining those of Taplow Court, give its chief beauty to one of the best-known reaches of the middle Thames.

4

But here, as so often, the Thames has but one side. The dreary flats of Whitebrook Common cover the Berkshire bank, with the suburbs of Maidenhead behind; and Cliveden only gets its prospect by turning sideways and blocking the view across the river by lofty trees. The original house was built by the notorious Duke of Buckingham, the friend of Charles II. Here he brought the Countess of Shrewsbury after killing her husband in a duel, while the Countess held his horse disguised as a page. The next distinguished occupant was Frederick Prince of Wales, who gathered here all the friends his father most disliked. But he had a taste for music; Horace Walpole notes the visits of many foreign instrumentalists to Cliveden; and here for the first time was performed Thomson's masque *Alfred,* which contained Dr. Arne's air of *Rule Britannia.* The house was burnt down in 1795, and again in 1849, after its restoration. It was rebuilt in 1851 from designs by Sir Charles Barry, and was for a time a residence of the first Duke of Westminster. It is now the home of Lord and Lady Astor.

Hedsor lies in the sharp angle of Nobleman's Corner, and the road to the left of it gives us the first public approach to the river between here and Taplow Bridge. The mansion of Hedsor, built by the first Lord Boston, equerry to King George III, is superbly placed on a northern spur, with views up the Thames Valley to the hills that close upon it beyond Marlow. On the far side, below a wood of yew trees, a deep ravine separates it from the main ridge upon which a sham castle, said to have been designed by King George himself, was erected by his faithful servant. Strangely enough, this ivy-covered imitation looks not unpleasing when seen, framed in trees, from the bottom of the valley. On the tip of the spur, below the house, stands a tiny church of flintstones, which has had incumbents since the year 1200. From the churchyard the view is magnificent. The house and park have lately been sold by the present Lord Boston, and the future of this commanding hill is doubtful.

Throughout our walk cross-roads have continually invited us northward to Beaconsfield: at no point have we

BEACONSFIELD.

been more than four miles from it, and from any we could have reached it through unspoilt country. It lies where two main roads cross, and each of these four arms gives off lanes on either side, so that had we walked northward up the ridge instead of striking across it from east to west we could scarcely have avoided being drawn into its web. The crossing forms the centre of the old town, dividing it into two long and two short arms, called Oxford End and London End, Windsor End and Aylesbury End, with the Market Place in the middle. In the wide, main street, you may see sitting side by side examples of all the good old styles from the days of Queen Elizabeth to the earlier Georges. Mr. Bathurst's drawings show us the tower of the church rising behind the corner of Windsor End, and, taken from about the same spot, Oxford End in the evening shadows, with the signboard of the " White Hart " standing out into the market-place; but he could have turned in almost any other direction and found rows of houses equally attractive. There is scarcely a discordant note from end to end. The church, which stands near the centre—a few steps up the Windsor Road—was practically rebuilt in successive restorations of the last century; but flintstones never look aggressively new, and the churchyard, with trees within and in the road without, adds an attractive splash of green to the street. The old Rectory, with two great gables framed in black oak projecting to form a little quadrangle in front, runs along one side of it; the arms of Burnham Abbey, lords of the manor of Beaconsfield, are above the doorway and fix its date before the Dissolution of the Monasteries. Beneath a fine walnut-tree near the churchyard wall rises the conspicuous monument to the poet Edmund Waller, who lived close by; but few will admire its design, or stop to spell out the long and laudatory Latin inscription that covers all the available space upon its sides. Within the church a simple brass upon the floor, with a tablet lately added on the wall above, marks the last resting-place of a greater resident than Waller— Edmund Burke.

The old town of Beaconsfield, like the country round

it, also owes its debt to rich men's habitations. Two large parks, to east and to south, run right up to its houses, saving the old from being engulfed by the new and preserving to it the restful character of earlier days. At the bottom of London End the gates of Wilton Park look straight up the broad main street, causing the London and Amersham roads to swerve to the right and the left. The present house was built in early Georgian days, with additions at the end of the century by the brothers Adam. Its park borders the London road for more than a mile. The property was purchased before 1780 by Josiah Du Pré, governor of Madras, and is still held by that family. Behind the church, extending from the Slough to the Wycombe road, and, southward, beyond the borders of Beaconsfield parish, lies the great park of Hall Barn, the home of Edmund Waller. The Wallers were settled at Beaconsfield as early as the fourteenth century and became a considerable clan in the district. In the sixteenth century one Edmund Waller, thirteenth child of the bailiff of Burnham Abbey, migrated to Coleshill, and there was born the poet, his grandson and namesake. The latter Edmund lost his father at an early age and owed much to his mother, a woman of great force of character. It was she who secured his election as member for Amersham at the age of sixteen, and in 1624 she joined with him in purchasing Hall Barn and Gregories. Mark Noble, the eighteenth-century antiquary, who gathered family traditions from the Wallers of his own day, gives a pleasant picture of the old lady: [1]

" What has always given rise to the idea that the poet Waller was a relation of the protector Oliver, was their always calling cousin, a usual custom at that time, where any family connexions were, though the parties were not actually allied; Mrs. Waller, the poet's mother, was a loyalist, and would often tell Oliver, that things would revert to their old channel, and leave him and his friends in ruin; upon which he would take up a towel, as his custom was, and throw it at her, saying, ' Well, well, aunt

[1] *Memoirs of the House of Cromwell*, by Mark Noble, 1787.

(as he used to call her), I will not dispute the matter with you ': but when his highness found that ' she was more in earnest than he in jest,' and that she held correspondence with the royalists, he put her under the custody of her daughter Price: but although the protector called Mrs. Waller aunt, and her son, the poet, cousin, yet there was no real relationship between them; the patriot Hampden indeed was first cousin to them both. . . ."

During her son's exile for his share in what is known to history as " Waller's Plot," she remained at Beaconsfield in charge of his children and estates. His daughter arrived at a marriageable age during his absence, and there was correspondence about her suitors. Of one the grandmother writes—" The young man is about 22 years old, yet he has buryed a wife. . . I can have him for £2000 ": but, she adds, " I am not in a hurry to marry hir, she is younge enough to stay but the danger is if she should catch the small poxe or hir beauty should change . . ." [1]

Beside the steadfastness and capability of the mother, the complaisance of the son cuts a poor figure. Edmund Waller celebrated the termination of his exile by a *Panegyric on the Lord Protector,* and five years later was penning a poem *To the King, upon his Majesty's Happy Return.* But his name will live for his lyrics like *Go, Lovely Rose,* and some of the verses addressed to his lost love " Sacharissa," sister of the murdered Algernon Sidney, sometime member for Amersham. Towards the end of his life he bought a small house at Coleshill: " a stag," he said, " when he is hunted and near spent, always returns home." But it was at Hall Barn that he died in 1687.

The house was rebuilt early in the following century by his successor, and the wood called the Grove to the south of it was decorated with an obelisk and statues. Noble, visiting the Wallers, found in it " one of the most elegant best-proportioned rooms in the kingdom, and perhaps the most poetical in the world, built in honour of

[1] *Victoria County History of Buckinghamshire.*

their ancestor, the poet." It contained portraits of the poet, his mother, and of the beloved Sacharissa, " with pearls of vast value appendant to it." The house remained in the Waller family till 1832, when it was sold to Sir Gore Ouseley. It was untenanted for a time, and required much restoration when it was purchased in 1880 by the first Lord Burnham, the creator of the *Daily Telegraph*. It is now the seat of his son, the second baron. The third great house of Beaconsfield, the Butler's Court of Edmund Burke, has long vanished. We shall pass its site when we walk to Penn.

Apart from these famous residents, the history of Beaconsfield centres in its road. In the earliest coaching days passengers from London to Oxford used to stop a night at Beaconsfield or Wycombe; and it was considered a remarkable feat when improved roads, better springs, lighter coaches, and faster horses enabled the journey to be accomplished in a single day. During the Great Civil War, when the King kept his Court at Oxford and London stood for the Parliament, there was much desultory fighting in between: and a great mound, said to contain the mingled bodies of Cavaliers and Roundheads, still stands as a *memento mori* on Beaconsfield golf links. For centuries these rough commons and thickets were the favourite haunts of highwaymen. " Beat a bush," runs the old Chiltern saying, " and its odds you start a thief! " The office of Steward of the Chiltern Hundreds, now only used for political purposes,[1] had its origin in the necessity that arose in very early days for checking the depredations of bandits among these wooded hills and valleys; and the three hundreds in question—Stoke, Burnham and Desborough—cover the Buckinghamshire portion of the Oxford road. Of the noted highwaymen whose names appear in Captain Smith's *Lives*, not a few

[1] A member of the House of Commons once elected is not allowed to resign his seat at will; but he is forced to vacate it if he is appointed to an office of profit under the Crown. A member wishing to resign is therefore said to accept the Stewardship of the Chiltern Hundreds, a post which now entails no duties but automatically causes the vacation of his seat.

THE WYCOMBE ROAD : BEACONSFIELD.

made their living near Beaconsfield and even within the town.   Jack Shrimpton came from Penn and used his local knowledge to good purpose: " he did always the most damage between London and Oxford, insomuch that scarce a coach or horseman could pass him without being robbed."   He was kind to his friends.   Once he met a farmer of his acquaintance being carried off to gaol by two bailiffs: he paid the debt and fees, and then, waylaying the bailiffs further on, recovered his own money with interest.   In the Crown Inn in Beaconsfield the famous Claude Duval joined a festive party, and, stampeding the company by a trick, robbed a farmer of a bag containing 100 sovereigns.

In 1794, after the trial of Warren Hastings, Edmund Burke applied for the Stewardship of the Chiltern Hundreds; and it was proposed to make him a peer under the title of Lord Beaconsfield.   But the death of his adored son Richard removed all desire for hereditary honours, and Burke died broken-hearted three years later.   It was out of reverence for Burke's memory that a statesman of the following century, who had no connexion with the place, selected Beaconsfield for his own title.

CHAPTER V

BY PENN TO AMERSHAM

THE direct road from Beaconsfield to Amersham leaves the great Oxford highway at the east end of the town near Wilton Park, and runs near Hunger Hill and Coleshill, which we have already visited. We can tap a new tract of interesting country if we strike north, ascend the hill to Penn, and making our way through great woodlands descend upon Amersham from the north. We start, then, from the central cross-roads by the church, and take the short northern arm of the old town called Aylesbury End. The name seems odd to-day, for a motorist going to Aylesbury would not hesitate to take the Amersham road; but in former days the traveller struck straight across the hills and joined the valley route at Great Missenden by the narrow road still called Windsor Lane, because it was once the customary route, through Beaconsfield, to Windsor.

Almost where the old town of Beaconsfield ends the new town begins; and, though some of us may regret the loss of green fields, a new generation will have little cause for complaint. The growing street follows the pleasant lines of the old lane and the red-brick houses are mostly well-designed. Only round the new station is the suburban character pronounced—a perhaps unavoidable result of rapid development—and everywhere possible the old trees have been left standing, so that from the hills above it escapes the effect, observable in similar circumstances elsewhere, of a red rash that has suddenly broken out on the green landscape. The chief cause for sorrow is that these houses on our left cover the site of the old home of Edmund Burke, the greatest inhabitant of Beaconsfield. Salt is rubbed into the wound in the further fields, where once he drove his plough, by enormous notice-boards offering little plots upon the " Burke Estate "; an action that seems as tactless as that of the amateur poultry-keeper who speaks of the boiled fowl upon the table by the pet name to which she has answered these three years within the poultry run.

Gregories was built by a rich London family called Gregory in 1704, when Londoners had already begun to find in Beaconsfield a place conducive to rest and health, and it passed to a branch of the Waller family. From them Burke purchased it in 1768, enlarged it and changed its name to Butler's Court. It was a purchase even more improvident that Disraeli's at Hughenden: Burke had to borrow nearly all the money, and his hospitality to visitors and generosity to neighbours kept him constantly in debt. When Mrs. Burke sold the property in 1812, the original mortgage of £14,000 was still upon it; the house was burned down in the following year and never rebuilt. But Edmund Burke loved it and found it convenient: it was but twenty-four miles from London and within an easy ride of his constituency at Wendover. Of his life at Butler's Court much has been written; how he kept open house, with creditors at his door, befriended the despairing poet Crabbe, or fed the poor with flour ground from his own corn in his own mill. His taste in friends was catholic. Dr. Johnson, the sage of Fleet Street; Reynolds, the painter; Dr. Burney, the musician, and his daughter the novelist; Garrick, the actor; Richard Shackleton, the Quaker; Fox and Windham, his political friends, and George Grenville, his political enemy: all were welcome, and at Butler's Court were equally likely to meet the exiled King and Queen of France or James Gomme, the Wycombe auctioneer. Less known is the account given by Arthur Young, the agricultural writer, of the visit he paid to Burke's farm and his opinions upon it.

It is clear that Burke took his agriculture very seriously and worked hard. That he actually drove a plough is proved by a good story related by Mr. Roscoe, which he in turn received from the grandson of the solicitor concerned.[1]

[1] *Between Thames and Chilterns*, by E. S. Roscoe.

This solicitor's clerk was sent to serve a writ on Burke, and seeing a man ploughing in a field near the house inquired if Mr. Burke was at home. " Mr. Burke is out," answered the ploughman, and the clerk returned without fulfilling his mission. The ploughman was Edmund Burke himself. Nor is it likely that his fields were less untidy than his house. They had no resemblance to the modern " pleasure-farm " which proud owners keep to display to week-end visitors: Burke's technical accounts of his experiments with wild parsnips or with rabbit's dung would have left such guests unmoved. But, when Arthur Young came riding half across England to see him, deep called to deep. Affairs of state might never have existed when they got down to discussions of draining fields or folding sheep. Throughout the whole account there is not a single word to show that Young realized that his host was the leading orator of his day and the chief inspirer of the Whig revival. They were simply brother farmers.

" From *Marlow*," he writes, " I crossed the country to Beconsfield; for the following particulars of husbandry around that place I am indebted to the very obliging attention of *Edmund Burke*, Esq. . . .

" Mr. Burke has been an arable farmer but a short time; he has however made so good a use of it, as to have formed several experiments, which will speak for themselves; but let me first insert the particulars of his farm, which will show that the scale of his husbandry is not small.

" 410	Acres in all	2	Carrots
160	Grass	1	Cabbages
160	Arable	2	Potatoes
90	Wood	3	Vetches
250.l.	Rent	6	Horses
40	Acres Wheat	14	Cows
25	Barley	6	Young Cattle
16	Oats	40	Swine
16	Pease	1	Man
25	Clover	2	Boys
25	Turnips	6	Labourers."

THE ROYAL STANDARD OF ENGLAND: FORTY GREEN.

A description of various experiments follows, of which the following are typical:

" DEEP PLOUGHING

" Mr. *Burke* ploughs in common from 10 to 12 inches deep: this being double what the farmers ever attempt, surprized his bailiff, who declared that his crops would be utterly ruined; but a regular and unbroken success in every one has convinced him, that deep ploughing is not so pernicious a practice as he apprehended.   The products have been better than those of the neighbouring farmers. Now this is a most material point, for if he has such crops at first he most undoubtedly will have great ones afterwards . . .

" DRAINING

" Ten acres of land were so very wet, that the crops produced by it were trifling.   Mr. *Burke* cut hollow drains across it, 18 inches deep, and three wide at bottom; some of them three feet deep, varying with the fall of the land; they were filled with chalk-stones, and some with bushes, the latter the cheapest: the drains answered extremely well, for the land has since been quite dry. . . .

" OXEN

" Oxen this gentleman uses in his tillage with great success; he works them in harness in the manner already mentioned to be practised by Mr. *Cooke* and Sir *Charles Tynte;* he uses three and one horse in a plough, or four oxen, and they do an acre a day; whereas the farmers plough no more land with from four to six horses; it is from hence very evident, that the practice must answer very greatly; it reduces the prices of tillage more than half.

" SHEEP

" It is the custom of this country to fold only the wethers; but Mr. *Burke* has regularly practised the folding his ewes as well as wethers, and without the least inconvenience to his flock. . . .

" These experiments are valuable, and cannot but be attended with very good effects to the husbandry of the neighbourhood; but the introducing the culture of carrots, the folding ewes, the use of oxen, and the practice of hollow draining can scarcely fail of proving highly important: these articles of management continued with the spirit, with which Mr. *Burke* will prosecute them, will by degrees bring his Tenants into the same conduct: the advantages that must result from such an imitation are many and striking. His country is much indebted to him for giving so laudable an attention to the improvement of her husbandry." [1]

The railway at Beaconsfield runs out of sight through a deep cutting, and the main road across the railway bridge goes forward to Penn by Knotty Green. But it is a good rule for a rambler never to take the straight road if he can find a crooked one. By cutting across to the narrow lane that passes the hamlet of Forty Green, we shall add little to the distance and shall have the opportunity of visiting a very interesting inn, the only one that bears the name of the " Royal Standard of England." We turn to the left down Baring Road, and, where it twists into Baring Crescent, continue along another road running in the same direction. A hundred yards beyond we enter Hogback Wood. Here again comes the sudden transition from town to country so typical of the lower Chilterns, for its acquisition by the National Trust has set this wood as an everlasting barrier against urban development. It was well worth preservation: on the rising ground silver birches mingle with the beech trees and there are good views of the Wycombe valley down the deep ravine up which the coaches used to toil, before the Holtspur cutting

[1] *A Farmer's Tour Through the East of England,* Vol. IV.

was made, to the great convenience of highwaymen. But
picnic-parties have already shown their appreciation by
leaving a trail of cardboard cups and paper. The lane
we seek borders the wood on the far side and we can
reach it by any path running over the hill. It is a very
narrow road with high banks on either side, made in the
days of pack-horse transport—as rural a route as any
lover of seclusion could desire. A sunny orchard alive
with scuttering piglets runs down towards it; little spinneys of high trees stand here and there; and an old farm-
house rises above us on the left where the road from
Knotty Green enters on our right, affording the best
approach for motorists. Just beyond, a few yards up a
side-lane on the right, stands the "Royal Standard of
England."

As you would guess from Mr. Bathurst's drawing, it is
a house that nobody could pass without stopping to look
at it. With its black timbers, mellow bricks and sagging
roof it might be almost any age. In the main building
there are signs of slight repairs where the old woodwork
has perished, but the flint portion adjoining can scarcely
have been touched for centuries. It is known to have
been an inn, then called the "Ship," three hundred years
ago, and how much longer nobody can tell. Passing
through a forecourt set with benches we step through the
door straight into the parlour, where a long rounded settle
faces a generous fireplace. We look about us; then sit
up and take notice. The old prints on the walls look
uncommonly good ones; the table in the centre is clearly
what dealers call a "period piece"; brass powder horns
of varied shapes are ranged along the mantelpiece. A ten-
stringed lute hangs upon the wall, and an old-fashioned
metal fire-blower—great-grandfather of modern bellows
—lies by the chimney corner. The place is a veritable
museum. The big round table with the inlaid star was
made in the seventeenth century and used to stand in the
old church of Beaconsfield; and if you pull up a chair
to the fire on a cold day, you may toast your toes at the
massive grate where Edmund Burke toasted his. It came
from Butler's Court.

There are many inns near London where dealers plant their antiques, which visitors buy at enhanced prices in the belief that they are securing a genuine old family heirloom. But there is nothing of that about the " Royal Standard." The host, Mr. Allison, is a born collector, and his treasures are the harvest of many years' devotion to the chase in sale-rooms and old houses. What you see in the parlour is but an *apéritif*: if he finds you appreciative he may invite you into the rooms behind. His love for good tables partly explains the crowded effect of the long low room with black rafters that lies within, but the tables are none too many to hold the wonderful array of things upon them. Lowestoft cups sit side by side with old English glass of varied shapes; Dresden china of many ages fills a shelf and needle-work pictures lean against the wall. It would take a week to give half of them the attention they merit. Pick up one of those simple-looking wooden wine coasters of the time of William and Mary and marvel at the craftsmanship that shaped it, the diligence that inlaid the beaded ornament. That piece of Coalbrookdale, 1746, would surely hold its own in any company. Did Hepplewhite ever conceive a more delicate wheat-ear than that which adorns a chair in the smaller room? A perfect writing-desk by the same master stands behind it. At the top of the long room, presiding over the close-packed treasures that fill it from end to end, stands a tall grandfather's clock. Its works were made by John Green and its case by Thomas Chippendale; its face is Battersea enamel. Not unnaturally the " Royal Standard " attracts many customers outside its regular local clientèle. You may find the host in a corner talking politics with a member of Parliament, or appraising the points of a new acquisition with a well-known connoisseur, or discussing the virtues of the beer he imports from Burton with a shining light of Harley Street. Many a collector whose money talks at Christie's has gone away discomfited. When his rooms are full to overflowing Mr. Allison may dispose of some few things to make room for more; he will sell a duplicate when he can get a better specimen; occasionally at a sale, when he

Charles J. Bathurst y S.

THE CROWN: PENN.

sees good things selling below their value, he may buy to sell again. But from the bulk of his collection, the pieces nearest to his heart, he will never be parted. " Yes," he will say, having just refused a king's ransom for some tiny treasure you could carry in your pocket, " he may be rich and I'm poor; but I like to think I've got something that his money can't buy."

Following the narrow lane upwards we come in a mile to Penn. As we reach the summit the lane widens out into an open space, with a great tree in the middle. To our left is the ancient church of Penn, to our right a row of attractive old cottages. In front, beyond the cross-road, is the picturesque Crown Inn, which Mr. Bathurst has chosen for his drawing; the ridge is here so narrow that the ground falls steeply from its back door, and past it we look straight down upon the widespread wood-lands of Penn House or, away to the right, across the valley to Winchmore Hill and the more distant Coleshill. Thus placed, the fourteenth-century church tower affords a wonderful all-round view, said to embrace parts of fifteen counties. Essex can be clearly seen on a fine day to the right of the London smoke; and, if we may take the dim outline of the Cotswold range to include the three counties on the further side that touch its summits, we can come somewhere near the number without great difficulty.

This end of Penn is but three miles from Jordans, and this propinquity has led many visitors to suppose that William Penn the Quaker was one of the Penns who had long made their home at Penn. This confusion is strengthened by the tombs in the church. In the south aisle are a number of interesting brasses depicting Penns of Penn in armour, with their wives and children, from the sixteenth century onwards; and a stone in the nave marks the vault in which six sons of Thomas Penn, " proprietor of Pennsylvania," and grandsons of the great William Penn, are buried. But the kinship between the two families has never been proved, and must, in any case, have been distant. In the Middle Ages Penn Church be-longed to a Northamptonshire priory, and after the Dissolution its advowson, with that of Little Missenden, was granted by King Edward VI to Sybil Hampden of Hampden, who had been his nurse and governess, on her marriage to David Penn, who had been barber-surgeon at the court of his father. They had property in Penn and lived in the old manor house along the road. In the days of the founder of Pennsylvania the heads of this family were their great-grandson William Penn of Penn, a country squire who had little concern with politics, and his son Roger, the last of the male line, on whose death in 1731 the Penn property passed to his sister Sarah, who married Sir Nathaniel Curzon of Kedleston.

On the other hand the descent of the great William Penn can be traced back through four generations to a certain William Penn of Minety in Wiltshire: and even if, as has been suggested, this early William Penn was a younger son of David Penn of Penn, the Quaker could only claim cousinship in the third degree. But that a relationship existed he never doubted, for on the tomb of his father, the Admiral, at Bristol he described him as " son of Giles Penn, of the Penns of Penn Lodge, in the county of Wilts, and those Penns of Penn in the county of Bucks." This, and the fact that the arms of the two families were identical, is strong presumptive evidence. That the Founder knew and had an affection for the place which carried his own name we cannot doubt: it was part of the country where he found a refuge among friends when treated as an outcast elsewhere, the home-land of his wife Gulielma. A hundred yards up the road beyond the " Crown " stands Pennbury Farm, and it can scarcely be a coincidence that when he built his American home on the banks of the Delaware he christened it Pennsbury Manor. A similar feeling must have led his son Thomas, who had joined the Established Church, to bring the bodies of his sons from Stoke Park for burial at Penn.

The village of Penn runs along the ridge and joins up with Tylers Green at the other end. There is scarcely a row of houses: they stand separately with bright gardens about them and few are younger than the eighteenth century. Many of them have been converted into summer residences for Londoners. On this road Edmund Burke

set up a school in 1796 for sixty young French " aris-
tocrats " who had lost fathers or near relations in the
Revolution. He visited it constantly from Beaconsfield,
supported it generously, and often brought food from
his own table for masters and pupils. The children all
wore uniform and had white cockades in their hats inscribed *Vive le Roi*; in the case of those who had lost
their fathers the letters appeared on a red label, of those
who had lost uncles on a black. The Marquis of Buckingham gave them a brass field-piece and a pair of colours.
Burke was most anxious to secure its continuance after
his own death: he commended it to the care of Pitt, and
a government grant of six hundred pounds was made each
year till the school came to an end with the Restoration of
1814. The field where the school stood was long known
as French School meadow.

The long straight road that follows the hill divides at
the pleasant three-cornered little common of Tyler's
Green. All along one side of the village run the extensive
grounds of Rayners, once the residence of the Rose family,
and now an institution. In the days of Queen Victoria
it belonged to Sir Philip Rose, a distinguished solicitor who
was for many years political agent for the Conservative
party and became, by Lord Beaconsfield's will, his exe-
cutor and trustee. A curious scene was once enacted here.
Queen Victoria last saw Lord Beaconsfield when he visited
Windsor in December 1880; he returned to Hughenden,
and died in the following April. Three days after his
funeral Queen Victoria went to Hughenden to visit the
grave of her favourite statesman, and decided to take the
exact route by which he had travelled when he last parted
from her. As it happened, he had called at Rayners to
see his friend and solicitor on the way. Similarly the royal
carriage left the main road at Loudwater and ascended the
hill. At the Loudwater Gate of Rayners it was met by
Sir Philip Rose's groom, who conducted it on Lord Beaconsfield's tracks through the grounds to the front door, and
so on to the gate at Tyler's Green leading to Cryers Hill
and Hughenden.

We must now return to the " Crown " by Penn Church

5

and take up the thread of our walk. Passing the inn we descend the hill to the left by a footpath which soon enters a lane taking us to Penn Bottom. We follow the valley to the left, narrow and well-wooded, for a mile, and then turn up a lane to the right where the trees stand still closer and thicker on either side. On our right are the grounds of Penn House, the seat of Lord Howe, the present representative of the Penns of Penn. The marriage of the Penn heiress to Sir Nathaniel Curzon has been mentioned; their grandson Penn Assheton Curzon married the co-heiress of Richard, first Earl Howe, the celebrated admiral, and a new grant of the Howe title was made to their family. Penn House stands well upon a rounded hill with close-cropped lawns and flower-beds about it; but its chief glory lies in the woods that clothe the lower slopes, pierced by avenues into which one passes immediately from the garden paths. A crown on one of the windows commemorates a royal visit by King Charles; a seat in the garden, brought from another residence of the family, is that upon which Handel sat to compose part of *The Messiah*: and on a spur to the south rises the old admiral's main-mast upon which his flag is hoisted on each recurrence of the Glorious First of June.

As we near the top of the hill our road emerges upon a long narrow stretch of green bordered by the village of Penn Street. We go straight forward by a footpath with the beechwood still upon our left, till we reach the church at the other end. There we turn left and follow a track through the spacious solitude of Penn Wood, coming out at last upon the Amersham-Beaconsfield road at Beamond End. From this road many lanes lead down to the valley at Little Missenden, but that which descends from Holmer Green is by far the most attractive. The road to Holmer Green is opposite us; we skirt the orchards of Beamond's End, cross a hollow, and then turn sharp to the right at the pond in Holmer Green. We descend along the side of a little valley, with trees upon our right and sometimes on the left, giving intermittent views of other woodlands crowning the opposite slope. Little Missenden lies athwart

Charles P. Bathurst del.

SHARDELOES.

the bottom of this subsidiary valley, on the banks of the Misbourne, with the long wooded ridge of Hyde Heath at its back. The village has kept its peacefulness by lying on a by-pass which leaves the main road at one end of the parish and rejoins it almost at the other, and has a happy old-fashioned air. From the corner where we enter the street the church and churchyard make a very satisfying picture. A considerable portion of the church is early twelfth century, and, apart from the porch, which was built in modern times of old material, the youngest part of it is the fifteenth-century tower. On the hill behind is Mantel's Farm, which Turstin Mantel owned in the days of William the Conqueror; so that Little Missenden enshrines many ancient memories.

The Manor House, which forms one wall of the churchyard, has had modern alterations, but is mainly of the early eighteenth century, with a Jacobean portion that can be seen beyond the churchyard wall. Most of it was the work of Dr. Benjamin Bates, physician to Sir Francis Dashwood, Lord Despencer, and himself a member of the " Hell-fire Club." His thorough respectability is the strongest evidence against the scandalous stories of Medmenham revels, and to the end of his life he stoutly maintained that, though members like Wilkes, Paul Whitehead, Charles Churchill or Bob Lloyd might drink too much, the general tone of the club was not unhealthy. Bates was a friend and patron of many artists and visited Rome with the sculptor Flaxman. When he built his long saloon (now divided), Flaxman adorned the apses at each end with panels in bas-relief; Angelica Kauffmann designed the charming terrace and balustrade outside and planned the garden, making skilful use of the water of the Misbourne.

We can avoid the main road by following the lane to the western end of the village; where the road turns to the left to cross the stream, we take a footpath forward that soon brings us into the park of Shardeloes and eventually comes out at the entrance to the town of Amersham. Mr. Bathurst's drawing gives an excellent impression of Shardeloes when the shadows fall across the park. It is

one of the few Chiltern manor houses that can be well
seen from the main road or railway. The property came
to the Drake family in the reign of James I by marriage
with a Tothill heiress, eldest of thirty-three children,
whose father had entertained Queen Elizabeth here. Their
descendants, the Tyrwhitt-Drakes, still own Shardeloes,
but the house was rebuilt in the eighteenth century with
the help of the Adam brothers. Many travellers have
recorded their impressions of the place. Bishop Pocock
in 1751 found it " finely improved in wood, lawn and
water "; and Cobbett, at a later date, cutting across from
Hertfordshire on one of his " Rural Rides," was so en-
grossed in computations of the value of its fine oak-trees
that he quite forgot to rail at the " rotten borough " of
Amersham. Stebbing Shaw came past when setting out
on his tour to the west of England in 1788. He had not
yet come to appreciate the new-fashioned Adam style, but
he gives a good picture of the wide power enjoyed in
Amersham by the squires of Shardeloes for many generations:

" The old seat was a noble one and remarkable for its
fine gardens. The present Mr. Drake has re-built it in a
manner much admired, but it does not seem to make a
great figure from the road. The park and grounds are
beautiful; the gentle swells of rich verdure crowned with
groups of charming foliage, and the lawn falling gradually
to the water's side, form the most picturesque assemblage
one can well conceive. . . . The borough of Amersham belongs to Mr. Drake, who, and his eldest son, are
the present members; the patronage of the rectory also
belongs to him, which is very valuable. I had almost
forgot to mention, that the parsonage house appears ad-
vantageously on the hill above the town, the present in-
cumbent doctor John Drake, the worthy patron's third
son. . . ."

With the passing of the Reform Bill Shardeloes could no
longer send two members to the House of Commons, but
that the influence of the family in local politics continued

is proved by an amusing letter printed in the *Life of Lord Beaconsfield*, by Messrs. Monypenny and Buckle. In 1858 the squire of that day wished to secure an East India cadetship for some friend or relative and wrote to ask Disraeli, then Chancellor of the Exchequer, to use his influence to that end. Dizzy sent an urgent note to Lord Stanley at the India Office:

". . . Read the enclosed, and help me in due season, I pray you! For the Tyrwhitt-Drakes to ask a service of me is the Hapsburgs soliciting something from a parvenu Napoleon. After thirty years of scorn and sullenness they have melted before time and events. Their formal adhesion to me would add immensely to my power in this part of the world."

It is possible that Disraeli was here touching on a mystery of the English country which he never fully understood. The implication of snobbishness is contradicted by all other records of the Drake family; indeed a mutual love of horseflesh is said to have led many of them into friendships with men of more humble antecedents than the Cabinet Minister at Hughenden. But they have been apt to divide mankind into those who ride well to hounds and those who don't: and Disraeli didn't. Their sporting tendencies were fully shared by the younger sons at the rectory, and many stories are still told of the hunting prowess of the last " Parson Drake." He was most punctilious in reading the service daily in Amersham Church, but on certain mornings there was a clink of spurs as he left the vestry and a glimpse of a pink coat and top-boots beneath his surplice; his hack was waiting at the churchyard gate.

The old main street of Amersham is perhaps the most satisfying street in all this Penn country. Like Beaconsfield, it has examples of all the good old styles of building, but its best houses are a little better and it has interesting features Beaconsfield lacks. Soon after entering the town we notice on the right the old almshouses, with their little brick courtyard and a row of pollarded trees in front. They were built and endowed in 1617 by Sir William Drake, who constructed the gardens at Sharde-loes, for six poor widows of burgesses of the town; and another Sir William Drake in 1690 erected the Market Hall which stands on pillars in the middle of the street near the central cross-road. Mr. Bathurst's drawing was made from the further side. The new town of Amersham has lately sprung up over the ridge to the north, around and beyond the railway station, well out of sight, and, with Chesham Bois, now forms a continuous town nearly extending to Chesham.

Amersham Church, where John Knox and Richard Baxter preached, lies up the side street to the north. From the outside its symmetry is somewhat spoilt by the addition of the Drake burial chamber and vestry, but the tower, standing out above the old houses, looks well from any direction. The chancel, burial chamber and vestry have many monuments of the Drake family. The opposite side was formerly devoted to memorials to the Brudenells of Raans, who owned the Shardeloes property in the reign of Henry VI, but few now remain. The fine old farm-house of Raans, red-brick with mullioned stone windows, is well seen on the right from the railway, as one travels from Chalfont Road to Amersham, at the point where the branch line curls away from Chesham.

In the old days Amersham was a great centre of Lol-lardy. Many local men were punished after the Lollard revolt of 1414, on the condemnation of Sir John Oldcastle, but their persecution was most vigorous in the years be-tween 1500 and the Reformation. Many Amersham Lollards were burnt at the stake, their relations being forced to carry the faggots and their children to light them. On the hill north-east of the town is a field where the burnings are said to have taken place, and there is a spot in the centre where the corn still grows more thinly. Some tiresome person made excavations during the last century and found an old chalkpit which had been entirely filled with flints; but the chalkpit would be visible to all the town and may well have been the place of martyrdom. The same fervour that inspired the Lollards found a fresh

AMERSHAM.

outlet when the Society of Friends gathered its first Chiltern adherents. There were many Quakers in Amersham, and Thomas Ellwood records a distressing scene that occurred when one of them, named Edward Parrot, was buried in 1665. A magistrate named Ambrose Benett lay in wait for the funeral party in the Griffin Inn, and, as the bearers passed, rushed out upon them with a drawn sword in his hand, attended by the constables, and commanded them to set down the coffin. He then " set his hand to the coffin, and with a forcible thrust threw it off from the bearers' shoulders, so that it fell to the ground in the midst of the street, and there we were forced to leave it." Many of the Quakers were arrested and the rest driven away. The body was left lying " in the open street and in the cartway; so that all the travellers that passed by, whether horse-men, Coaches, Carts or Waggons, were forced to break out of the way to go by it, that they might not drive over it, until it was almost night."

We have only one other house to visit. Right at the end of the town, at the corner of the Beaconsfield road, stands Bury Farm. Its straight front, facing the road, is of later date, but the old brick gables at the back remain from the original building. This was the " Berrie House in Amersham " where Ellwood found lodgings for Mary Penington and her children, when Bottrells above Chalfont St. Giles proved " too strait and inconvenient " for the family. It is a landmark in the Penn Country, for here Gulielma Springett first met William Penn.

CHAPTER VI

THROUGH THE DISRAELI COUNTRY [1]

CHIPPING WYCOMBE, to give High Wycombe its official title, greatly took the fancy of old William Camden in the days of Queen Elizabeth, and we can well believe in the beauty of its situation before modern developments brought its rank crop of red-brick suburbs. " This town," he writes, " for largeness and beauty, compares with the best in the county; and, as it is governed by a mayor, is justly preferred to the rest." Its early fame as a market, to which it owes its distinctive name, is easily explained by its position. It stands at the point where the main valley, running up from the Thames at Bourne End, first divides. To the north runs the Hughenden valley, which, dividing and subdividing into many " bottoms," eventually emerges by innumerable routes on the summit ridge crowned by Hampden Common and Hampden Woods. To the north-west the main road runs on to West Wycombe and here other divergences occur, one valley forming an easy pass for road and railway to the vale by Princes Risborough while others lose themselves in the complicated ridges between Radnage and Lane End. All these bottoms converge on the great thoroughfare of Wycombe, and make it the natural outlet of a wide stretch of Chiltern country.

Camden's idea of " largeness," applied to a town, was widely different from ours, and the Wycombe of his day is probably represented by the inner core clustering round the church, which is now the only picturesque portion of this manufacturing town. The church itself is a very

[1] Any writer on the Disraeli country must necessarily acknowledge his indebtedness to the standard *Life of Lord Beaconsfield* by W. F. Monypenny and G. E. Buckle.

fine one, dating originally from the reign of Edward I. The tower, which is the outstanding feature of the town as seen from all the hills around it, was built in 1522 by Roland Messenger, the vicar. His architectural skill must have been noted, for he was chosen by Wolsey to take charge of the construction of the tower of Christ Church, Oxford. Apart from this, Messenger is chiefly remembered for his zeal in burning heretics. The most conspicuous monuments within are the elaborate eighteenth-century tombs of members of the Petty family, Earls of Shelburne: but the most pleasing epitaph is to a lady who " preferred to be, rather than to seem, learned."

The fine broad High Street, like those of Amersham and Beaconsfield, is typical of the old Chiltern towns. There are many good eighteenth-century houses in it with some of vastly earlier date, and the former Town Hall, rebuilt on pillars by Henry Earl of Shelburne in 1757, projects forward to give distinction to the western end. Opposite is the curious little Market House, of circular shape, and the great tower of the Church rises proudly above the line of houses on the right. The Red Lion Hotel belonged for centuries to Brasenose College, Oxford, and its portico, with a veritable Red Lion standing life-size upon it, was the scene of a dramatic incident in Disraeli's first Wycombe election in 1832. His opponent was Colonel Grey, son of the Prime Minister, who was genuinely " unused to public speaking." Dizzy records the event in a letter to his friend Mrs. Austen:

" Yesterday," he writes, " the Treasury sent down Colonel Grey with a hired mob and a band. Never was such a failure. After parading the town with his paid voices, he made a stammering speech of ten minutes from his phaeton. All Wycombe was assembled. Feeling it was the crisis, I jumped up on the portico of the Red Lion and gave it them for an hour and a quarter. I can give you no idea of the effect. I made them all mad. A great many absolutely *cried*. I never made as many friends in my life or converted as many enemies. All the women are on my side and wear my colours, pink and white. . . ."

Wycombe people assert that the Lion itself played a part in his harangue: that he pointed to its vermilion head and said, " When the poll is declared, I shall be there "; then, indicating its tail—" and my opponent will be there." Colonel Grey returned to the charge and won the day; but five years later, when Disraeli was returned for Maidstone, the citizens of Wycombe made a subscription to illuminate their town.

Rows of brick villas now stretch for several miles along the main road, east and west of High Wycombe; up the valley to the north the flood is only stemmed by the fence of Hughenden Park, and houses of various sizes and styles cover the hill to the north-east, above the railway station. Only on the south has Wycombe breathing-space, where the grounds of Wycombe Abbey School creep up the hill to meet the late Lord Lincolnshire's well-wooded park at Daws Hill. Wycombe Abbey, the old manor house of the town, was never a real abbey, and its name till recent times was Loakes. It was purchased in 1700 by Henry Petty, first Lord Shelburne, and in the days of his great-nephew, the Prime Minister, had many eminent visitors. Nor were they all Tory politicians. John Wesley greatly admired the grounds: " What variety," he writes, " in so small a compass! " and the French abbé Morellet found here as his fellow guest that versatile genius, Benjamin Franklin. During Franklin's earlier visit to England he must have met Lord Shelburne, who became Secretary of State in the very year when Franklin's diplomacy secured the repeal of the obnoxious Stamp Act. The ambassador-scientist had now returned with other American commissioners to discuss terms of peace and the recognition of the United States, and he had many private conversations with Shelburne. One is glad to think that his time in the Chilterns was not all spent in diplomatic negotiations. " I saw him there," writes the abbé, " make the experiment of calming the waves with oil, that one has looked upon as a fable in Aristotle and Pliny. It is true that they were not the waves of the sea, but those of a little river that flowed in the Park at Wycombe. It was ruffled by rather a fresh wind. He ran back about two hundred steps from the place where we were, and, making some magical gestures, he shook three times over the stream a flask which he had in his hand; a moment after the little waves weakened and calmed down by degrees, and the surface of the water became smooth as glass."

Shelburne was valued by his colleagues but gained (somewhat unjustly) such unpopularity in the country that no Government dared make him again a Minister. In compensation he was created first Marquess of Lansdowne, and, retiring to a country life at Bowood, sold Loakes to Robert, first Lord Carrington. The Caringtons —who dropped an " r " in the surname to avoid confusion —retained the Abbey till 1896, when, selling the house and a portion of the park to become the home of a highly successful school for girls, they retired to Daws Hill, which sits pleasantly on the summit of the ridge behind. The old gateway, which formerly stood at the entrance in the High Street, was moved to the end of the new drive near the top of Marlow Hill.

From High Wycombe, in a not too strenuous day's walk, we can visit Hughenden, Bradenham and West Wycombe, and we need scarcely touch a high road all the way. A convenient motor-bus from the middle of the town, addressed either to Great Missenden or to Speen, will carry us quickly through the red-brick and plaster barrage to a spot named Crossways, where an incipient street on the left soon becomes a country lane. This would eventually lead to the village of Downley up a subsidiary bottom, which serves to isolate a spur wholly occupied by the demesne of Hughenden. But our way lies over the spur. Entering the park by a gate where a notice prohibiting bicycles predicates the existence of a public footpath, we follow the drive up the slope, till, near the summit, the footpath strikes off across the grass on the right to Hughenden Church. The church stands well on the hillside, surrounded by great trees which here, as elsewhere in the park, command our admiration; a pleasant streamlet runs in the bottom. But the almshouses by the churchyard seem to be the only links with the past, for the church itself, after many restorations, gives no outward clue to its genuine antiquity. There are a few old monuments within, but the general impression is of a Beaconsfield mausoleum. Over the pew where her favourite statesman always sat Queen Victoria placed her tribute, with the text, " Kings love him that speaketh right "; and outside the great east window, filled in his honour by undergraduates of the University of Oxford, is the vault in which the great man was laid to rest. On either side lie the two women who admired and helped him—Mrs. Wyndham Lewis, who became his wife and was made a viscountess at the request of her grateful husband, and Mrs. Brydges Willyams, of Torquay, whose legacy of £40,000 enabled Disraeli at long last to clear Hughenden from mortgage. Close by is a tablet to the Prime Minister's brother, Ralph, whose son is the present owner of Hughenden. A road curving round the churchyard takes us up the hill, passing close between the house and its gardens and stables before descending to the hollow beyond.

The Hughenden estate had notable owners before it was purchased by Benjamin Disraeli. Before the Conquest it belonged to Queen Edith, daughter of Earl Godwin and wife of the Confessor, and passed later to Odo, bishop of Bayeux, whose martial figure, clad in black armour with white collar out of respect for his cloth, may be seen in needlework at Bayeux laying about him with his mace at Hastings. The Black Canons of Kenilworth held it till the Reformation, when it passed to the Dormer family, and descended to Philip Dormer Stanhope, Lord Chesterfield, whose letters to his son throw so lurid a light on the practices thought proper for a young man of fashion in his day. But the house occupied by these early owners stood on a different site from that of the present building. The first mansion on this particular ridge was built by a subsequent purchaser named Savage. He was followed by the Norris family, who lived here till John Norris died in 1845, leaving it vacant for Disraeli's occupation two years later. The price of the property was £39,450, and Benjamin Disraeli and his wife could only lay down £15,000 in ready cash. His father helped him a little, but the bulk of the money was advanced by the Bentinck brothers, sons of the Duke of Portland, for political reasons. The Tory party sadly lacked a head with brains inside, and Lord George Bentinck had complained that he had found them a marvellous man as leader whom they would not accept because he was not a country gentleman. The ample means of the family enabled them to remedy this deficiency.

The present mansion bears little resemblance to the white, many-cornered house which Disraeli bought, as it is depicted in a painting that hangs on the walls of Hughenden to-day. The long rectangular building now visible has no particular architectural charm; its bright red bricks seem to be of the unfortunate texture that never tones with age. But it looks comfortable, with big windows to catch all the midday sun, and attractive views between the trees are obtained from its terraced lawns. Inside the Victorian atmosphere is carefully preserved. Birthday presents from Queen Victoria lie here and there, including terra-cotta statuettes of her favourite retainers, and her portrait by von Angeli enjoys a place of honour. There are other interesting portraits both of the Disraeli family, from Lord Beaconsfield's grandparents onwards, and of many of his political and literary friends. That of Lord Chancellor Lyndhurst, the patron and friend of the young Disraeli, painted by his other early friend, Count d'Orsay, once belonged to Gladstone, who sold it at Christie's. It was eventually purchased and presented to Disraeli by a number of his colleagues in Parliament. The library remains much as Lord Beaconsfield left it, and books innumerable cover its walls, as became his father's son.

The transformation of the house was gradual. Various stages are described by Disraeli in letters to Mrs. Brydges Willyams. "The chief business of Mrs. Disraeli, during this residence," he writes in 1858, " is to adorn the Terrace in the Italian style "—with vases specially imported from Florence: and again, in 1863: " We have realized a romance we have been many years meditating:

we have restored the house to what it was before the Civil Wars, and we have made a garden of terraces, in which cavaliers might roam and saunter with their ladye loves." His accounts of how he set about his task of becoming a country gentleman—attending Quarter Sessions, opening an infant school, giving a servants' ball—are cynical and amusing, but that he had a genuine love of certain aspects of rural life, that he fully appreciated the songs of birds and the changing aspects of the Chiltern woodlands, is proved in many a passage:

" We were absent nearly a fortnight, and I find a great difference in the colour of the trees—the limes all golden, the beeches ruddy brown, while the oaks and elms and pines are still dark and green, and contrast well with the brighter tints. But not a leaf has fallen; they want the first whisper of the frost, and then they will go out like lamps when the dawn breaks on a long festival."

Resuming our walk in the lane behind the house we descend the hill under the shade of lofty trees. Looking through a gate on our right we note broad woodland paths following the contours of the hill by easy gradients. These were planned by Lady Beaconsfield, who planted conifers and laurels among the beeches beside them; her husband, with memories of similar set walks at Ems or other German watering-places, called the wood his " German forest." Passing through a gate at the foot of the hill we follow a cart-track across an open field, and then ascend through a corner of the beechwoods, which, having kept company with us at a little distance on the right, swing back in graceful curves to meet us. Emerging from the shadow we enter Downley Common, a long expanse of close-cropped turf, upon which we can walk, touching no road of any kind and meeting no fence, till we emerge on the village green of Bradenham some four miles further on. From the gate of the wood a broad hollow lies before us, and little islands of cottages, set by twos and threes in little enclosures, and almost

HUGHENDEN FROM DOWNLEY COMMON.

hidden by the orchards about them, rise here and there on the slopes of the smooth green down that surrounds them. Ascending the steep slope to the right we bend upwards towards the old smithy that sits picturesquely beneath a giant tree near the summit of the ridge. Turning back to face the way we have come, we enjoy an attractive view of Hughenden peeping through its trees and mellowed by distance. As so often happens in approaching the Chilterns from the south, we find that, almost without noticing the climb, we have attained a considerable elevation. Hughenden, which looks to stand so high from the road by which we started, now lies in a hollow, barely showing above the fringe of beeches just below us. The ridge behind High Wycombe rises far above it to the horizon; rolling beechwoods converge on either side; and the whole, with the bare downland in the foreground broken by a few stunted thorns and a tuft of cottages, makes a typical picture of Chiltern scenery.

The metalled road, which arrives at the smithy from another direction, comes to a full stop before it, but the track that runs forward across the grass follows the line of an ancient highway once much frequented by highwaymen. Down this slope Queen Elizabeth came riding one sunny morning with her lords and ladies, guided by Lord Windsor of Bradenham, her host of the previous night. She was returning from a State visit to her University of Oxford, and descended by steep Hobbes Lane behind us to receive an address from the loyal burghers of Wycombe. As we follow her trail backwards we pass an invisible point where Downley Common becomes Naphill Common and soon the open down gives way to thick clumps of bracken and furze and hawthorns; gradually beech trees rise on either side to hide the outer world, and the glades between show a singular diversity of vegetation that places Naphill in the front rank of Chiltern commons. Oaks mix with the beeches. Birches show their silver trunks against a patch of hollies, and junipers spring up, not one by one as elsewhere, but in solid grey-blue companies. Marooned among the beechwoods which terminate every vista we may light upon a couple of thatched cottages with no semblance of a road to guide them to civilization: here and there a stagnant pool reflects the peaceful scene. Smooth broad rides invite us in all directions, but eventually we must curve to the left —the west—and taking one of several converging tracks through a solid beechwood emerge in a patch of fairly open country. Passing on our right three groups of lofty trees, each group surrounded, unexpectedly, by a circular earthwork, and on our left the great clearing of Bradenham Manor Farm, we descend steeply past a pleasant keeper's cottage to the back wall of the Manor itself. Avoiding it to the left we follow the side wall downwards, with glimpses over of silent walks between high walls of dark evergreens, and come out on the village green of Bradenham.

Bradenham sits just as an English village should do. Along the far side of the green runs an irregular row of houses, all different but all in keeping with the picture. At the bottom, where the main road lies, a farm with great barns and rickyards ends the line; and, in the place of honour at the top, the fine old church and the red-brick manor house sit side by side in amity, as Church and State should do, with widespread beechwoods topping the hill behind. Here in 1829 came Isaac d'Israeli, author of *Curiosities of Literature*, and from this base his eldest son, the future Lord Beaconsfield, fought his earliest election battles.

In the greater fame of his son, whose reputation for political sagacity and foresight never stood higher than it does to-day, the important position held by Isaac d'Israeli in the world of letters is often forgotten. He was a close friend of two poet laureates, Pye and Southey: and Lord Byron devoured every word he wrote. Bulwer Lytton was also a fervent admirer, and when John Murray, the publisher, fed his lions, Isaac d'Israeli occupied an honoured place at the table. It was to Pye that he owed his first introduction to the county. Having fallen on evil days, Pye had been provided with a cottage near Stoke Poges by John Penn, a grandson of the first proprietor of Pennsylvania, who was then living at Stoke Park, and there he welcomed the elder d'Israeli as his guest. In 1825 the family came to the upper Chilterns, renting for the summer months Hyde House, half-way between Great Missenden and Chesham. Sitting at the end of its avenue of ancient trees, Hyde House looks from the road a gloomy residence; but the southern side, with garden and paddock surrounded by a half-circle of perfect beechwoods, provides all the beauty and seclusion any writer could desire, and here young Benjamin Disraeli wrote the greater part of his first novel, *Vivian Grey*.

The reasons that induced Isaac d'Israeli, in the evening of his life, to desert Bloomsbury Square and the attractive neighbourhood of the British Museum Library for a permanent Chiltern residence are set out by him in a letter to Southey: " The precarious health of several members of my family has decided me upon this movement, and I quit London with all its hourly seductions. My house is described by the ' Nourisse of Antiquitie,' venerable Camden, as built by the Lord Windsor in the reign of Henry VIII—for the salubrity of the soil and air." Hither were carted all his books, and here he gradually went blind and died. Books were always the ruling passion of his life: " The Octavos," he writes, " are my Infantry, my Cavalry are my Quartos, and the Folios are my Artillery." Everybody liked him. Mrs. Wyndham Lewis—the future Lady Beaconsfield—whose first husband had just succeeded in getting her second elected as his colleague at Maidstone, came to Bradenham and fell at his feet. " I have been paying a visit," she writes to her brother, " to Mr. Disraeli's family. They reside near High Wycombe—a large family house, most of the rooms 30 or 40 feet long, and plenty of servants, horses, dogs, and a library full of the rarest books. But how shall I describe his father: the most lovable, perfect old gentleman I ever met with? " Many years later Lord Beaconsfield pictured Bradenham—with a good measure of novelists' licence—as the " Hurstley " of *Endymion*.

In those days Bradenham Manor had another interesting inmate in Giovanni Battista Falcieri, Lord Byron's private gondolier in Venice, who remained with him as

6

his devoted body-servant till his death. He is immortalized by a couplet in *Don Juan*:

> " Battista, though (a name call'd shortly Tita),
>   Was lost by getting at some aqua-vita."

After fighting in the Greek War of Independence, Tita was discovered by Dizzy's friend Clay in Malta and accompanied the two young men on their Oriental tour. His next engagement is foreshadowed in Benjamin Disraeli's letters to his sister. " Giovanni called on me (announced by the servant as *Don Giovanni*). He has left Clay and brought me a lock of Byron's hair from Venice, which he cut himself off the corpse at Missolonghi." Then, a month later—" I saw Tita to-day, who suggests that he should return with me to Bradenham and try our place." To Bradenham Tita came, and he must have caused something of a sensation in that particularly English village. He remained as a privileged retainer till Isaac d'Israeli died, when he confessed that he had already married the English housekeeper. His subsequent disposal was a matter of some difficulty, but Benjamin Disraeli used his influence to obtain for him a post as messenger in the Government service, and, after his death, a pension for his widow. Tita's portrait hangs in distinguished company at Hughenden.

Bradenham has another title to fame from its connexion with the Bradenham hams—black without but rich and luscious within—which one sees in the windows of the more expensive provision dealers. The recipe was the private property of a family named Mason, which throughout the eighteenth century held the Mallards Court portion of the neighbouring manor of Stokenchurch, and had its family vault beneath the little Norman church of that village. In due course it passed to a Mason descendant, sometime high sheriff of the county, who lived at Bradenham Manor not long before the Disraeli era. During this sojourn, a faithful butler married an equally devoted cook, and as the reward of good service they were given a copy of the recipe with full permission to make use of it for commercial purposes. They are said to have prospered exceedingly and their " Bradenham " hams won public recognition.

We have touched no highway since we started, but must now follow the main road towards High Wycombe for half a mile, when we pass through a gate on the right and arrive, under a railway arch, at Averingdown Farm. Straight from the farmyard a footpath leads upwards to the shadow of the woods, and we follow it as it curves to the left till we reach the summit of the hill. Following the path across a cultivated clearing and through a fringe of woodland we emerge on open down and see the ridge on which we are walking tapering to a point before us. Right on the tip, its steeple surmounted by a great golden ball, stands the curious church built for the people of West Wycombe by Lord Le Despencer of West Wycombe Park, better known as Sir Francis Dashwood, founder of the so-called " Hell-fire Club " at Medmenham Abbey. Wilkes, the politician and pamphleteer, who first entered parliament in 1757 as member for Aylesbury, visited it not long after its erection, and describes it in a letter published in Almon's biography.

" I am just returned from a tour in Buckinghamshire," he writes, " which has afforded me much pleasure . . . I returned by West Wycombe, and passed a day in viewing the villa of Lord Despencer, and the church he has just built on the top of the hill for the convenience and devotion of the town at the bottom of it. I must own, the noble lord's gardens gave me no stronger idea of his virtue and patriotism, than the situation of the new-built church did of his piety. Some churches have been built from devotion, others from parade or vanity; I believe this is the first Church which has been built for a prospect."

Dashwood had been selected, curiously enough, as Chancellor of the Exchequer in Lord Bute's short and unpopular administration; Wilkes was no longer friendly to him, and is scarcely fair in his criticism. Dashwood's place of worship, of which the tower was erected in 1761 and the remainder completed two years later, was built on the site of a much earlier church, and the earthworks that surround it indicate a very ancient occupation of the hill point. But proofs of his eccentricity are not wanting. The inside of the church is simply a great hall, and comfortable arm-chairs took the place of the usual pulpit and reading-desk. The ball on the steeple contains a room where twelve people can sit. Wilkes suggests that it was made convenient " for the celebration not of devotional but of convivial rites," and calls it " the best Globe Tavern I was ever in "; but, as the only egress is by an outside ladder descending dizzily to the very edge of the tower, any potations enjoyed within could hardly fail to be moderate. Still more remarkable is the Mausoleum outside the end of the church. It has no roof, being simply an hexagonal plot of grass surrounded by great walls of brick and flint with many openings through them and niches within designed to receive the burial urns of Dashwood, his family and his friends. It was erected by Dashwood with money left him by his friend Lord Melcombe Regis, to whom it is dedicated in a prominent inscription. The building has no beauty—it looks unfinished—but standing within and looking at the view framed by the entrance archway, one recognizes that it, too, was built " for a prospect." Church and Mausoleum are exactly aligned to point down the long straight road that follows the Wycombe valley to the great tower of High Wycombe Church, and then forward till it climbs Holtspur Hill to be lost in the woods of Beaconsfield. The road has widened; building since the war has practically obliterated any gaps between West Wycombe and High. The great meadow, where the earlier citizens of Wycombe came out to enjoy the hanging of malefactors, is covered with furniture factories and the homes of their employees. Yet still to-day, particularly in the dusk of evening, one must concede that it is " a prospect."

Standing before the Mausoleum one can enjoy from the selfsame spot a second prospect. Turning right we face the still more attractive view which Mr. Bathurst has chosen for his picture—the dark-red roofs of the old street of West Wycombe peeping through the trees below us with the ancestral home of the Dashwoods rising in its park behind.[1] Wilkes's gibe at the gardens had a double edge. He had just visited Stowe, where the grounds were adorned with temples to Ancient and to Modern Virtue and with statues of British patriots; and Dashwood is said to have so laid out his park with plantations, streams, paths and clumps of trees as to represent in outline the female form divine. Another curious conceit won the approval of Arthur Young when he passed through in 1767. He tells us that on the lake before the house "floats a ship completely rigged, with a long-boat, and another lying alongside: her masts rising above the adjoining trees in a manner which adds greatly to the landscape." But these eccentricities of Sir Francis have long since passed away and it is possible to admire whole-heartedly the peaceful view without any such extraneous distractions.

We descend the steep slope of turf before the Mausoleum and strike the road at the top of Church Street—surely the most curious Church Street in the country. The hill is precipitous, but the way does not descend in zigzags, like approaches to hill-top shrines in Italy or Southern France. It falls straight and steep, the door of one cottage on a level with its neighbour's bedroom window, till it emerges at the bottom through an archway beneath the attractive old Church Loft into the still unspoilt main street of West Wycombe. "Was St. Paul to preach in this Church," comments Arthur Young, " he must furnish the neighbours with more than mortal legs to become his auditors "; and there is little cause to wonder that a new church has been built at the foot of the hill.

The steep grass slope which descends to the road at the Oxford end of the village is one of the few places where one can enjoy winter sport out of season. On any summer's evening you can see a host of boys and girls careering down the hillside on toboggans at quite a creditable speed. Most of the village children possess their

[1] See frontispiece.

own craft, which you see sitting outside their cottage doors, but if you wish to join them you can hire a toboggan from an old lady in Church Street for two-pence. The West Wycombe type is neatly made, with smooth wooden runners, and one sits upright and in luxury upon a little seat covered with a strip of carpet. The sport seems to be peculiar to this place and its date of origin is unknown.

West Wycombe street wholly belongs to the past,[1] though the tentacles of the new High Wycombe press close upon it. There is a sharp transition from old to new at the fork where the London road divides to Aylesbury and to Oxford, and here, like an outpost of the past, a curious eighteenth-century column of stone, surmounted by a ball, serves at once as a milestone and a signpost. On three of its four sides is written—" From the City 30 miles," " From the University 22 miles," " From the County Town, 15 miles." Instinctively one attributes the work to Sir Francis Dashwood. In its shapeliness one sees the taste of the founder of the Dilettanti Society; in its studied periphrases the hand that wrote the recondite mottoes at Medmenham; and in its erroneous figures the calculations of Lord Bute's Chancellor of the Exchequer. Here, far more than in church or mausoleum, we recognize the true memorial to the much-maligned father of the Medmenham Club.

[1] Early in 1929, after this chapter was written, a signal honour was paid to West Wycombe by its selection for purchase and pre-servation by the Royal Society of Arts as a typically beautiful English village. When its sale was first mooted, a proposal was made by American admirers of rural England that it should be bought and bodily transferred to the United States. But however carefully this task might have been accomplished, West Wycombe would never be the same without its steep hill above and wooded park below, and one may be grateful to the Royal Society of Arts for its retention.

CHAPTER VII

FROM GREAT MISSENDEN TO THE VALE

FOR exploring the upper heights of the Middle Chilterns Great Missenden is as good a centre as any. The railway, which first invaded this peaceful valley in 1892 and brought the village within an hour of London, creeps unobtrusively up the hollow and has not destroyed its rural charm. Distance has proved sufficient to save the place from conversion into another great dormitory for the City, and the survival of private estates, keeping the horizons inviolate, leads one once again to join King Solomon in his praise of " rich men living peaceably in their own habitations." On all sides the view is bounded by woodlands. Where the valley takes its graceful curve below the village, the wall of firs and beeches that crowns the Abbey park descends to meet the more distant woods of Shardeloes and Little Missenden on the opposite slope. To the north the estates of Lee Manor guarantee the same immunity from Vandalism, and from the hill above the church one gazes westward straight up the long avenue to Hampden House, with Hampden Woods on either side and beyond. Up the slopes on both sides of the valley run footpaths which, in a short walk, take one into a land of deep woods and sunny commons which might well be a hundred miles from any centre of population.

The place-name means the wooded hollow by the river Misse or Misbourne, and, as the birthplace of the stream that waters Angelica Kauffmann's garden at Little Missenden, and furnished the lake at Shardeloes and the mediæval fishponds at Chalfont Park, Great Missenden deserves all credit in a land where water is so often the one thing lacking to an otherwise perfect view. But the actual source of the Misse is not too easy to discover. Not so long ago a gentleman came to inspect a house in the lower part of the village, tempted by the agent's description of pleasure grounds " sloping down to the banks of the river Misbourne." He found no river, but in its place a dry ditch some six feet wide, choked with weeds. Nevertheless he took the house, and some seven years later he was kneeling on his library table, just above high-water mark, fishing for his books in the turbid river around him. The Misbourne in fact, like other chalk streams, has an intermittent flow in its upper reaches. Its original source appears to have been beneath the woods of Hampden, whence it helped to scour out the valley that leads to Chequers, but not since 1774 has it owned this parentage. The incident of that year is thus described by the then Rector of Hampden in his parish register:

" N.B. Early in ye Spring, in 1774, the Springs made their appearance in Hampden Bottom & rose to a far greater Height than in 1764; from below the Gravel Pits, thro' West Field, a large Stream of Water, thirty feet wide, bent its course by Riggnall during the months of March, April and May, & emptied it Self into Mobwell below Great Missenden. Tradition informs us y^t ye like happened 110 years ago."

To-day, in normal times, springs rising in the lake of Missenden Abbey, south of the village, form the visible source of the stream and the bed above is dry; but occasionally, through exceptional rainfall or some collapse of chalk obstructing its underground channel, the water rises at Mobwell, north of the village, and resumes its earlier course. Such an occurrence is always said to presage disaster. A flow in 1912 gave rise to scepticism, but the Great War came in the nick of time to restore waning faith and rout the heretics. The flow of 1917, which brought the big flood, was mainly caused, and enormously augmented, by a water spout that descended on the high ground toward Chesham, and scored a deep channel down the hillside. Amid the many disasters that have since assailed us, its exact significance is disputed.

The best view of Missenden Abbey, the big house of

THE MISSENDEN VALLEY FROM MARTIN'S END LANE.

the place, is obtained from a footpath that leaves the London road on the left at the end of the Abbey grounds, and, crossing the Misbourne, leads uphill to the church. Of the old abbey of Austin Canons, founded by the d'Oyleys in 1133 and endowed in 1293 by William de Missenden in gratitude for his escape from shipwreck, no part is visible, though some of the existing walls are of great antiquity at their base and carved stones are found embedded here and there. The mansion of the Fleet-woods, which followed the Dissolution, has also dis-appeared, and the building owes its present shape mainly to James Oldham Oldham, a worthy and wealthy iron-monger of London, who bought the property in 1787. He did much good in Missenden, repairing the church and building a school and vicarage; and his active support of the Countess of Huntingdon's Connexion gave a strong Evangelical tinge to many subsequent vicars. But the antiquity of the site is proved by the towering elms that border the road and the wide spread of the cedars by the house; and the wonderful close-cropped hedge of beech, box and yew, rising higher than the Abbey itself, was not planted yesterday. In such surroundings, with the lake in front and green lawns behind it, the view of the house from the Warren makes a pleasant picture on a summer's day. It has belonged to the Carrington family for more than a century.

The position of the church above the village, set firmly on a spur half-way up the hill, won praises from more than one eighteenth-century traveller before Robert Louis Stevenson, strolling through the woods from High Wycombe in the autumn of 1875, supplied the perfect description.

"Great Missenden was close at hand," he writes, "in the trough of a gentle valley, with many great elms about it. The smoke from its chimneys went up pleasantly in the afternoon sunshine. The sleepy hum of a threshing machine filled the neighbouring fields and hung about the quaint street corners. A little above, the church sits well back on its haunches against the hillside—an attitude for a church, you know, that makes it look as if it could be ever so much higher if it liked: and the trees grew about it thickly, so as to make a density of shade in the church-yard . . ." [1]

The church itself has been frequently restored, and close observers have found in it traces of every style that has prevailed from the eleventh century to the present. It has a good tower, though the avenue of elms that led to it is now reduced to four trees, and the two old porches on the south side have a certain charm. Within, the grey timbers of the roof and the view of the font and west end from the chancel, when the great west door stands open on a sunny day, are very pleasing. Some of the monuments are interesting. The two oldest are the fragments of fifteenth-century brasses on the wall by the Abbey pew, one in memory of John Iwardby and his wife Katherine, daughter and heiress of Bernard de Missenden, and the other to one Christopher Metcalfe, his wife and son. Both have an odd feature in common. In each case the bereaved husband erected the memorial at the time of his wife's death, and recorded upon it his own decease, leaving blank spaces for the day, month, and year. Both were clearly the last of their race to remain in the neigh-bourhood, for no pious descendant ever came to fill the gaps, and blank they still remain. Three good monu-ments of stone commemorate a seventeenth-century in-cursion of the Kentish family of Boys, who lived for generations near Canterbury and were intimately con-nected with its cathedral. All three members—repre-senting three generations—died here between 1632 and 1637; but their tablets were separated in a restoration of 1900, and the most interesting, that to William Boys, was skied above the south door to such a height that the in-scription is mostly unreadable. A fellow of Clarehall, Cambridge, his scholarship is indicated by his memorial, for the lettering is flanked and crowned by an arch of some sixty volumes—carved in marble and coloured—fat quartos in massive bindings that would make Dr.

[1] *An Autumn Effect.* Now included in *Essays of Travel.*

Rosenbach's mouth water. Opposite, over the north door, is the tablet to his niece Ann, wife of Thomas Eayrs, of Great Missenden, and right away in the north-west corner is the inscription to his aunt Lady Jane Boys, who, " after 23 yeares widdowhood, being aged 73 yeares, yelded to the separation of Soule and Bodye the 12 of Febr: 1635." This good lady left £100, the income from which she originally intended to be devoted to teaching poor children of the parish to read; but, " observing how very careless and neglectful parents were in sending their children to school " she diverted her benefaction to the putting out of poor children as apprentices.

The last memorial to be noticed takes uncommon pains to conceal its interest. It is dedicated to the Reverend Richard Marks, " 24 years vicar of this parish whose singular and eventful history recorded by his own pen in the ' Retrospect ' and various other writings has been made a blessing to thousands." Reference to this not too accessible work is required in order to learn that Great Missenden can boast of a vicar who fought as a combatant at Trafalgar. His books appear to consist of sermons converted into essay form, and contain here and there scraps of autobiography. " I was among the very first," he writes, " who received promotion from the Commander-in-Chief after the close of the battle of Trafalgar, in which the D—— took no minor part "; and, as his captain was " Sir G. H——," we can identify his ship as H.M.S. Defence (Captain George Hope) which formed one of the advance squadron which found the enemy and, in the actual battle, was thirteenth in the line commanded by Collingwood. After the war Lieutenant Marks, R.N., took Holy Orders and he came to Great Missenden in 1822. Though in general he is inclined to express regret for his unregenerate days in the Navy, and for the bellicose feelings that led him to be the first in boarding enemy ships, yet at times, when parishioners annoy him, the old fighting spirit shows through:

" As a Christian, the writer would not willingly or unnecessarily give offence to any: but in a work like the present he can no more think of softening down the truths of God's word and providence to meet *their* approbation than he can think of sending an apology to Napoleon Bonaparte for having formerly assisted in destroying the combined fleets of France and Spain off the hills of Trafalgar."

Having thus relieved his feelings, one pictures him sitting down pacific and repentant to continue one or other of his more popular works—*The Cottage Girl* or *The Thatcher's Wife* or *Pious Harriet*.

A stranger in rural England wishing to find the local footpaths would always be well advised to try an old churchyard. We have come to the church by one; and another leaves it on the same side, running up the hill through the Abbey park. It leads eventually to Hyde Heath, and, traversing the whole length of Hyde Heath common, forms by far the most alluring route to Chesham. For those requiring a short stroll another footpath is not far off. The steep road that runs past the church is enclosed by gates at top and bottom, in order that the vicar, if he be so minded, may still enjoy his ancient privilege of feeding his sheep upon its verges. The upper gate gives access to the highway where the roads to Chesham and to The Lee diverge. Take the latter, and a hundred yards on, where the main road turns sharply to the right, follow a lane straight forward. It soon ends in a footpath which, descending through fields to the main street near the station, gives a good bird's-eye view of the village and enables the stranger to form a general idea of the country we are about to traverse. Up the valley to the right the main road and railway take the summit at its lowest height and descend to the vale of Aylesbury at Wendover. To the left a wedge of wooded upland divides it from a secondary hollow, at the head of which the old home of John Hampden stands conspicuous among its trees. This leads to two higher passes to the vale, that on the right bordering the park of Chequers, the rest-house of Prime Ministers, while the other, climbing still higher through beechwoods, leads to a glorious prospect of hills and plain as, untrammelled by walls and hedges, one swings down Longdown Hill, and so forward to the Risboroughs, Thame, and Oxford.

Missenden High Street still has many old houses, and tall elm trees frame the view as one leaves it at either end. Inns with hanging signs are numerous. In the picturesque courtyard of the " George " stands the long timbered court house of the ancient manor. The " Buckinghamshire Arms," on the opposite side, has recently been converted into a bank, but its exterior has been wisely left alone and the old features have been retained within. It has been said by Mr. Clement Shorter and others that this was where Robert Louis Stevenson found his lodging, but there are many reasons for transferring the honour to the " Red Lion " across the street, a new-fronted house which betrays its antiquity within and at the back. Stevenson's landlord, it will be remembered, was the driver of the coach which ran to the " Bell " in Holborn, and old residents still remember a noted whip named Thurogood as host of the " Red Lion." Moreover, the writer went *up* into the sloping garden behind the inn, which fixes the house on the western side of the street. Coaching died hard in Missenden. Till the Great War the Old Berkeley Coach used to leave the " White Lion " opposite on periodical journeys to Rickmansworth. Its brave appearance and the merry sound of its horn gave infinite pleasure to many who never rode upon it. It tootled at the tennis club and the players stopped their rallies to wave their rackets in response; it tootled its respects to the sporting squire of Shardeloes; and the old street of Amersham, which had seen the rise and fall of the golden age of coaching, again echoed the familiar sound. It cheered despondent golfers hunting their balls in the prickly jungle of Chorleywood Common, and it was still tootling happily as it swung down the hill to Rickmansworth Station. But to-day the vast increase of motors on the road and changes of fashion have caused the Old Berkeley to seek new routes and the Misbourne valley is the poorer for its departure.

From Missenden Stevenson went to Wendover, as we

propose to go to-day. He walked up a chalky lane, then climbed a steep hill by footholes cut in the turf, and so arrived at his memorable picture of Peacock Farm, where peacocks were feeding with barnyard fowls in a sunny amphitheatre of beeches. Various commentators have suggested various routes, but to me it seems probable that he kept to the valley for some distance—possibly stealing a surreptitious lift—and only climbed the hill when he came near Wendover. But all memory of Peacock Farm has vanished, and the vagueness of the directions absolve us from attempting an R.L.S. pilgrimage. The distance is little over four miles, so that we can afford to diverge in search of pleasant paths. Let us then start towards Prestwood up the hill above the station. Passing the Green Man Inn at the top of the hill—in the Chilterns we direct by means of inns, which mostly stand at corners and display their signboards on high posts by the road so that he that scorches may read the pictured name—we see the first sign of a particularly Chiltern industry which we shall come across many times while we wander within the orbit of High Wycombe. Close by one of the cottages stands a wooden hut with an aperture at one end through which projects part of a long wooden pole with its end loosely tethered to a post. This is one of the humble workshops where the rough trunks of beech-trees are converted into chair legs and rungs, and the pole, which, in all, measures some fourteen feet long, is the primitive source of power for the work of turning. To the inside end of the pole is attached a string which is fastened to the treadle of the lathe and also twisted round the roughly shaped piece of wood upon which the craftsman is working. When the treadle is pressed and released by the foot the ends of the pole revolve rapidly and the wood in the lathe revolves with them. The finished articles are stacked outside the hut. Their perfect shape compels admiration, and the rapidity with which they are turned out is evidence of a natural gift for woodwork inherited from a long line of Chiltern craftsmen. The legs, with their stretchers, are collected by the furniture makers of High Wycombe, are there fitted with elmwood seats and such backs as are required, and sent, piled high on lorries, to many of the best-known shops in London. The shavings are collected in sacks and sold for kindling.

We turn from this ancient Chiltern industry only to find a new one. Leaving the main bus route at the next cross-roads we follow a curving lane to the right and soon see two great chestnuts holding their twin umbrellas over a little white gate on the right. A trim strip of lawn with gay flower-beds beyond leads to the picturesque farm-house of Pankridge, the headquarters of the Gaybird Game Farm. This is a good example of an industry which, originating within recent years in this particular corner of Buckinghamshire, has already attained sufficient success to exert a beneficial influence on rural employment. At Pankridge alone some 130,000 pheasant eggs are sold annually, and about 15,000 pheasants are reared and brought to maturity. The work entailed keeps twenty hands permanently employed, and the purchase of food and the provision of the long lines of wooden fencing for the pens also bring work and money into the district. Apart from the land owned by the firm, additional fields are rented annually from surrounding farmers, owing to the necessity of rearing the young birds on fresh ground each year. This enables the farmer, certain of his profit on a portion of his holding, to concentrate his energy on the improvement of the remainder. More pheasants mean more private gamekeepers, and beaters' wages in the autumn come as a welcome catch-crop to the labourer. Altogether, to an extent not realized by the dwellers in towns, the rich man's pheasant is rapidly becoming a far from negligible part of the poor man's livelihood.

The old orchard at Pankridge has been wired in to form an aviary, and here strange pheasants indigenous to many distant corners of the globe wander about in perfect amity with peacocks blue and white. Golden and silver pheasants flash across a patch of sunlight into the shade of the cherry trees, where their cousin, the Lady Amherst, displays an aristocratic difference in tail and hood. The giant Monaul, waddling uncouthly through the grass, seems well content to have left his native Himalayas, and

Reeves's pheasant, conspicuous in yellow and black, proudly extends his superior length of tail. There seems to be no end to the varieties, and our choice falls in turn upon the red-legged Swinhoe richly clad in blue shot silk, upon the delicate silver pencilling of the lineated pheasant, and upon the gorgeous Argus, with great peacock eyes staring from every patch of his body. A visit to Pankridge when the birds are in full plumage removes any regret that still lingers for the loss of Peacock Farm.

Returning to the road we keep straight forward past every by-way, passing the schools on the left and Moat Farm on the right, and then, crossing a road at right angles, take to the fields. Diving into a sunken lane and emerging on the opposite bank we enter Hampden Woods. A monument placed outside an upper corner records the fact that we are on historic ground: " For these lands in Stoke Mandeville," it begins, " John Hampden was assessed in twenty shillings of Ship money levied by the command of the King without the authority of law." But our path slopes downward to the right, and crossing the edge of an arable field we enter the great glade of Hampden House. So thickly is the glade overgrown at this point with giant bracken and self-sown oaks and hazels that its presence is not apparent until one looks up and sees the wall of trees in front; but a few steps to the left up a side path bring us into the open and we see Hampden House on its hill a mile away at the head of its majestic avenue. The unlikely story is still told that Queen Elizabeth, when she came here to visit Griffith Hampden, grandfather of the more famous John, complained that the high trees obstructed the view from her window. All the woodmen of the district were hastily gathered, and owing to their all-night labour Her Majesty on rising in the morning looked out upon the glade we see to-day. One feels that the Queen would not have thanked him for the disturbance of her night's repose: in deep woodlands like these the tap of an axe echoes like a footfall in a cathedral, and the Hampden giants fall with a crash to waken the dead. Close before us elms and sweet chestnuts alternate in the front rank on either side, and the beeches beyond, spaced and aligned in perfect order, were obviously also planted of set purpose. Far more probable is the other tradition that the drive that runs northward across the park to meet the Risborough road was specially made to shorten the royal route from Oxford. The glade from Hampden House terminates in a gateway on the road flanked by two curious round lodges locally known as the pepperboxes. The occupant lives and eats his meals at one side of the gate and retires to bed on the other.

Resuming our original path we soon emerge into the Missenden-Risborough road at Hampden Bottom, and, taking the lane that branches off beyond the old smithy opposite, climb the long hill to Little Hampden. A typical Chiltern " bottom " crowned with beechwoods lies below us on the right and the roofs of the half-dozen farms and cottages that form the nucleus of the hamlet show among the trees above us. Near the summit, the tiny church of Little Hampden stands on the left of the lane, backed by four tall fir trees. Described by the historians of the county as a " mean edifice," one visitor at least has found something very pleasant about it. The plaster that covers the old flint walls has toned to suit the greenery around, and the porch of two stories on the north side, its plaster framed in massive timbers bent by nature and roughly shaped by man, cannot fail to delight the lover of ancient things. The nave dates from the first Plantagenets, chancel and porch from the Wars of the Roses, and the ingenuous simplicity of the whole speaks eloquently of the continuous and unaided effort of humble woodlanders to do honour to their Creator. Within the church a small stone figure of an unknown bishop with crosier is embedded in the wall and some interesting wall-paintings have been recently revealed. In these wild thickets, a sinister significance attaches to the *two* representations of St. Christopher, for to gaze upon St. Christopher was held to ensure the beholder from sudden death upon that day. At the top of the hill the hedges that bound the lane draw apart. A few houses are scattered in a rough line to the left of the road, leaving a wide green

7

expanse to the right with two great walnut trees in the middle and woods behind. At the inn, which ends the village, the metalled road ceases and a grassy track goes forward through a bottle neck and along the whole length of Little Hampden Common. A gate at the far end, on the left, leads into a rough farm lane which rejoins the highway near Chequers.

To those who knew the village green and the common beyond in earlier days a walk across them in this autumn of 1928 would bring sadness. An unfortunate dispute early in the year has had disastrous results. The trouble seems to have arisen through the action of a few among the many motorists visiting Chequers at week-ends, who chose to return by the rough lane and across the bumpy grass of Little Hampden Common. This in itself was inconsiderate. A mint of money has been lately spent upon the main road, which runs nearly straight; there are many good rounds on tarmac surface to vary the return journey; and, though an old highway runs across the Common—a perfectly good highway when all travellers went on foot or horseback—it would have been a graceful act on the part of motorists, who have driven those who walk for pleasure off so many favourite roads, to have left this grassy route to pedestrians. But where one motor goes others follow, and soon, on a Sunday, motorists were driving all over the common and the green, breaking down brushwood and leaving behind them the débris of their luncheons. The lord of the manor, as I understand, took legal advice, and enclosed the track in iron posts and fencing, as so many farmers have been forced to do, for the same reason, on the hitherto open downs in Sussex. The villagers, probably not understanding the whole difficulty, were up in arms. Letters in the local papers attracted the attention of the sensational London press. The very name of " Hampden " roused all would-be defenders of liberty: the " Little " intensified the appeal to their hitherto latent chivalry. A crowd of Londoners, roaring and hooting through the quiet village streets in cars of every description, swooped down on the common by night and, " with dauntless

breast, the little tyrant of the fields withstood " by pulling
down the fence, breaking a few of the uprights, and
leaving the wire lying in unsightly heaps on the grass.
To what purpose? To-day the broken wire still lies
about the place; the posts are all still there, a few pros-
trate, some reeling like drunken men, but most of them
as they were planted. The villagers, delivered from serf-
dom, are beginning to throw out broken kettles and
dirty tins to join the rotting banana-skins of the Sunday
luncher. In former days this Common was particularly
clean, with close-cropped herbage. Wandering in the by-
ways among the golden gorse and blossoming hawthorns
one found many a tethered goat fulfilling his task with
the efficiency and rapidity of a motor-mower. To-day no
living thing grazes there. Thistles and rank grass already
nearly hide the gorse and the foxgloves, and floating
thistledown threatens a larger crop next spring. I give
everybody credit for good intentions. But Little Hampden Common, once conspicuous among the quiet beauty-
spots of the Chilterns, has lost its charm and, if no remedy
be found, will soon become an abomination.

But it is time to continue our walk. In order to arrive
at the required point it is necessary to descend to a lane
in the hollow on our right, which is now growing more
shallow as it nears the summit ridge. We have a choice
of ways. If we go back to the inn we shall find a well-
worn path opposite leading in the required direction; but
the wood that makes so fine a background at the north
end of the common is more attractive, especially when
the wild cherry blossom shines among the beeches in the
spring, or the foxgloves colour the undergrowth in early
summer. Passing through the gate in the middle we find
a track which descends into a hollow and then, curving to
the right over the opposite hill, enters the same road
further on. I doubt if there is any right of way; but
half the footpaths in England are private property and
only used by others through the courtesy of the owners.
No one is likely to stop the well-behaved wayfarer who
keeps to the path, lights no fires, breaks no boughs and
leaves no litter. The road, having risen gradually from

the valley, is now running upwards in a slight depression, and soon becomes level with the ground on either side. On the left a vast arable field seems to stretch for ever; to the right the thorny thickets of Scrubwood limit our view. Arriving at a T-shaped cross-roads we pass through the gate opposite and enter a common, part of the property given to the National Trust by Lord and Lady Lee of Fareham at the time when they presented Chequers to the nation as the country home of its Prime Ministers. Rolling clumps of gorse and bracken, blue-green junipers and stunted thorns still bound our horizon, as we follow the path to the right through low-growing heather; but rising above the brushwood we see the goal that is to make the climax of our walk—the golden ball on a pedestal that surmounts the monument to the Buckinghamshire men who fell in South Africa. Right up to the pillar the gorse rises high above our heads till turning a sharp corner we emerge into the sunlight, and look about us with genuine surprise. Close in front the ground falls steeply some six hundred feet and all the kingdoms of the world seem to lie before us. Beneath our feet the vale of Aylesbury stretches like a map with lines of poplars bordering its ditches, villages of toy houses, embowered in lofty elms, set here and there, and isolated little farm-houses, each in its tuft of orchard, standing among great fields of divers colours. Behind, the white tower of Aylesbury Church rises on its gentle eminence, and, as a background to the whole, a long green ridge runs up and down from Whitchurch to Quainton Hill, from Waddesdon to Brill, from Forest Hill to the Faringdon uplands, with the top of Wytham Woods peeping through the Oxford pass at Wheatley. Far to the right Mentmore shines white among its trees on the Bedfordshire border. Away to the left the rich lands of the plain extend far across the Thames to fade away in the distance like the sea.

Turning sharp left we have before us what is probably the best view obtainable from a public place of the historic manor house of Chequers. The south front can be seen clearly, at a distance, as one comes by road from

Great Missenden; but there the elaborate new gates and lodges in the foreground have not yet grown mellow, and the straight processional drive, devised by statesmen new-returned from a long sojourn at Versailles, seem not too happy in this undulating English park. From Coombe Hill no recent embellishments disturb us. The house is well seen through a gap in the lofty trees that stand about it, and here better than anywhere can we view the surroundings that give this house its particular *cachet*—the astonishing variety of spreading beechwoods, open downs and deep secluded valleys contained in the Prime Ministers' little triangle. High above rises the bold promontory of Pulpit Hill, on the top of which the energetic climber will find a camp of immemorial antiquity. Nearer to the house is the lesser eminence of Cymbeline's Mount, an easier Sunday walk for elder statesmen. It, too, has its ancient earthworks, and a foreign diplomat, by merely revolving slowly on the rampart, would enjoy a not unflattering epitome of southern England.

Turning our backs reluctantly upon Chequers, we follow the edge of the escarpment down a gentle slope towards Wendover. The green down is good walking for a well-shod traveller, but the multitude of tiny thistles causes dogs to tread delicately. The glow-worms seem to like it and may be seen here by the score at dusk on a warm summer's evening. They shone, as I remember, with particularly fervent loyalty when we ascended these hills on two Coronation nights to add our puny bonfire to their illuminations. At the end of the ridge the descent becomes precipitous and needs careful negotiation, for the chalky clay is very slippery after rain. We have scarcely become accustomed to the better foothold on the hard high road beneath when we arrive at Wendover Station.

CHAPTER VIII

GREAT HAMPDEN AND WHITELEAF CROSS

UNLIKE the Chess and Hughenden valleys on either side, which break up into innumerable lesser hollows spreading fan-like into a wide stretch of upland country, the valley of the Misbourne keeps itself to itself throughout its course. The watershed is never far from the stream, and the bottoms that descend to it are consequently short and steep. If we leave the valley at Great Missenden and strike a little south of west, we quickly ascend to the plateau occupied by the straggling parish of Prestwood, and in less than a mile and a half reach the first of the many ramifications of the Hughenden Valley. Here a wide choice of deep dales or narrow ridges lies before us, and by following any of them upwards we can attain the summit ridge. The stalwart walker can go straight ahead, pursuing a switchback course across the whole system. He can descend into the first valley between Stoney Green and Hampden Rectory and climb the other side to Denner Hill; slither down the slippery slope beyond and up again by another footpath which, by the map, bids fair to bring him quickly to Speen, only to find another deep ravine to cross before he attains that village. Speen will not detain him long. Its core is sound. The old post office at the cross-roads, with its adjacent cottages, is real old Chiltern, but new villas on the outskirts fail to maintain this standard. Even now he has not finished with the Hughenden Valley. Speen stands on a spur, and the deep hollow behind it is even more sharply cut than that before. Our Chiltern lanes are seldom turned aside by gradients, but this descends and rises by hair-pin bends, and right in the bottom of the pit sits the picturesque little Plough Inn, where a versatile soldier-writer-connoisseur, having restored and furnished it to his taste, dispenses hospitality to all comers. The narrow lane from North Dean becomes (not inaptly) something of a Pilgrims' way on fine Sundays when London visitors drive out to test the host's capabilities in his new rôle of publican. The hill above is stiff, but it is the last; thence the road runs fairly level to Lacey Green, overlooking the great gap that runs from Princes Risborough to High Wycombe. Such a walk would be no bad introduction to the Mid-Chiltern country: it shows, as well as anywhere, the peculiar folding of these hills on their southern slope, and he who has accomplished it cannot fail to admit that the Chilterns provide sufficient exercise in no great distance as measured by the map.

On the other hand, those who wish to save undue exertion will miss little by taking a bus for a mile and a half from Great Missenden station to the " Chequers " in Prestwood. I add " in Prestwood " because, if local tales be true, a certain confusion has occurred between this little inn and a house with a similar name some three or four miles away. We are told of great plenipotentiaries of foreign powers who have arrived at Missenden Station and hired a car to take them to Chequers. When the car stopped, they alighted, expecting a welcome from the Prime Minister of England, but, instead, found themselves admitted to the parliament of the elder statesmen of Prestwood. Be this as it may, at the " Chequers " in Prestwood we alight, and by walking straight forward past the inn we can find a route that coasts round the many heads of the Hughenden Valley, as on the rim of a bowl, and takes us to the summit ridge by imperceptible ascents. The directions are simple. Follow the curving lane to four cross-roads, and forge straight ahead, with beechwoods on the right, till it descends a hill. Here take a pleasant footpath on the left, which emerges on the road again near Hampden House. This is the key road, the guide to an infinity of varied walks. It takes you by many twists and turns to the further end of Hampden Common, and then, on a steady curve, through glorious woodlands to the Pink and Lily Inn above Princes

Risborough. Half a dozen lanes and tracks slope down from it on the left, each descending to its own valley or following an intervening spur; while others to the right lead one, almost on the level, to various points on the steep escarpment overlooking the great Vale below.

These are the two extremes. There are many walks in the Hampden country both for the weak and for the strong. But to-day we will follow a route that partakes of both, and zigzag here and there as the fancy leads us. If we disdain the aid of the motor-bus through Prestwood, we can find a parallel footpath more pleasant than the hard high road. Crossing the railway bridge to the north of Great Missenden Station, we turn sharply to the left and then, beyond a row of cottages, turn to the right again to find the little Nonconformist graveyard on our left. We can now go straight ahead for two miles and more through fields and woods, only crossing such roads as we encounter to enter an answering footpath on the opposite side. We follow a cart-track which vanishes before us in the shadow of the beechwoods and ascend a typical Chiltern bottom. At the top we cross our first road amid a cluster of new houses, an offshoot of the old hamlet of Martin's End. This with other hamlets has been in recent years incorporated in the new parish of Prestwood. The church lies a mile away to the left, the schools a mile on the right, and between the groups of old flint and brick cottages and scattered farms there has been much building of late. Some of the new houses are admirably designed and well suited to the country, but these are mostly of a retiring nature and lie up by-roads or hidden among orchards. Those that show their faces to the main roads are less happy, and, if they possess any style at all, sit incongruously by their neighbours, some frankly urban, some suburban, and others too intensely rural to ring quite true.

We keep these at a certain distance when we have crossed our second road and stretch our legs across the broad open fields that once were Prestwood Common. The larks still sing above us as incessantly as they did to R. L. S. when he crossed this ridge more than fifty years

ago and christened it the " Country of Larks," and the
cherry orchards, glorious in their spring blossoms and
still more striking when they turn to dark crimson, scarlet,
or flaming yellow in the autumn, according to their
several kinds, distract our eyes from the less successful
works of man. The wind blows upon our right cheeks:
we shall have a fine day. The local prophets would have
reached the same conclusion from more recondite evidence
—the behaviour of sheep, or a gathering of rooks upon
a certain meadow. One can understand more easily their
belief that " the Wycombe hooters make rain," for our
Chiltern weather is ruled by the prevailing wind, and, if
it blows from the south-west sufficiently strong to tell us
the furniture-makers' dinner hour, a wet day is almost
inevitable. A north wind may, in winter, bring a short
and sharp blast of sleet, but the day, in general, will
be fair. Definite traces of folk-lore are hard to find in
the Chilterns to-day, but the local elders are largely
guided by ancient axioms in verse or prose. We sow pars-
ley on Good Friday, regardless of the month in which the
Easter festival may fall. If you wish to have some
noxious weed eradicated the moment it appears in spring,
you will probably get some answer like

> " Don't pull in May.
> Wait till another day."

And if you try again a little later—" Ah, but they always
say

> " Pull in June,
> Pull too soon."

I may have been unfortunate, but I have never yet met
with a local adage equivalent to the business man's " Do
it now."

A short length of new road, which will probably soon
be a street, brings us out on the main road to High
Wycombe. The Chequers Inn is at no great distance to
our right and here the bus-riders can join us. We have
passed the area of new building and now enter undiluted
country. We take the short green lane immediately facing
our point of arrival, cross a stile and soon pass through
a gap in the hedge to our right, where a path runs diagon-

ally across a field to meet the corner of a larchwood in the hollow. This wood is known locally as the Cathedral Wood, and the path that runs upwards through it undoubtedly gives the feeling of a lofty aisle in some old cathedral. The larches are set so close that their trunks rise bare to a great height on either side; and in springtime, when the oxalis pushes its leaves of incredibly vivid green through the fallen spines beside the pathway and the young shoots on the topmost tips of the trees are seen as in a mist through the delicate tracery of the lower branches, a walk in the Cathedral Wood is well worth a far more serious divergence from our line. Where the pathway forks at the top of the hill we bear to the right and descend to a stile in the right-hand corner whence a path conducts us to a lane in the bottom. The road to Denner Hill ascends the opposite slope, but we turn to the right and keep up the hollow past the end of the road from Prestwood, till a path, marked by a great stone, leads us upwards through the wood upon our left. We cross and recross the drive that leads to Hampden Rectory and only turn into a field at the garden gate to skirt the garden and enter a lane beyond.

The impression given by Hampden Rectory is of complete seclusion and peace. The little lane which leads to its principal gate goes no further, and the main road from which it diverges, connecting Hampden Row with the rest of the parish, is in itself a *cul-de-sac*. Great trees stand round the house to east and west and north; on the south one looks past the cedars in the garden down a glade of meadows and pastures with never a house in sight. The Georgian south front is an addition of a later age that delighted in big windows to catch the sun, but the part we see through the gate, built in warm red brick that has faded to yellow in patches, with a gable above the door, must surely have sheltered the rectors of the troubled times when the patron, John Hampden, fought for English liberty, and the timber work on the end wall suggests an origin even more remote. Here came in 1637 William Spurston, appointed to the living by John Hampden, who, having lost his dearly loved first wife three years before,

became a close friend and confidant of his rector when he
retired worn out by strenuous days in parliament to seek
a respite in his country home. When matters had passed
beyond his moderating influence, Hampden enrolled his
tenants and neighbours in his famous regiment of Greencoats, and Spurston left this peaceful Rectory to become
its chaplain and follow its fortunes in the field. He was
present at Chalgrove on that fatal day in June 1643, and
ministered to his patron in his last hours at the little house
in Thame. Among the might-have-beens, few questions
have been more often discussed than the probable attitude which Hampden would have taken had he lived to
see the trial of his King: but we surely get a valuable clue
from the career of Spurston, who was so deep in Hampden's confidence and so thoroughly shared his views.
Spurston became Master of Catherine Hall, Cambridge,
but was dismissed from that post because he signed a protest against the trial of King Charles and refused to admit
the legality of a government " without a King or a House
of Lords."

If Spurston's best-known actions occurred away
from Hampden, his successor, Robert Lenthall, was the
central figure in a terrible tragedy enacted within the
Rectory walls. It all began with a happy little domestic
incident: the rector's fourteen-year-old daughter, who
was living in London, came down on a short visit to her
family. The country was still unquiet, and there must
have been general rejoicing at her successful accomplish-
ment of the difficult and dangerous journey. The sequel
is recorded in the Parish Register by her father's own
hand, and reads like another chapter in the Book of Job:

" 1647—My daughter Sarah Lenthall was buried ye 11th
day of August *an: supra,* she came fro London to Wickham & on ye Saturday only to see us, & so to returne y^e
morrow in ye afternoone to Wickham againe, but she fell
sick, and on Wednesday morning following, being ye 11th
of Aug: about an howre before Sun rise died of ye sicknes
and so in ye Evening we buried her in ye meade, called y^e
Kitchen-meade, by ye hedgeside, as you go downe into it

on yor left hand, a little below ye pond at ye enterance into the meade: she was aged 14 yeares eleven moneths seaventeene dayes, had she lived to Bartholomew day she had bin full 15 yeares of age.

"Susanna Lenthall, my wife, depted this life Thursday evening about 8 a clock ye 26 of August. She died of ye sicknes comfortably and in peace and was buried ye 27 by hir daughter Sara. John Gardiner a child y^t lived in my house died of ye sicknes and was buried August ye 29th.

"Adrian Lenthall my sonne a hopefull yong man & neere one and twenty yeares of age deptd this life, of ye sicknesse Thursday morning a little before day breake & was buried at ye head of his Sister Sara's grave, ye same day being ye 2nd of Septmbr.

"My cosen John Pickering a lad about 13 yeares of age dying of ye sicknes was buried the 25 of Septemb: 1647."

Though the plague only appears in the pages of history at times of extreme virulence, as in 1665, it was never absent from London. Many Chiltern villages maintained a pest-house, where vagrants from the city, upon whom suspicion fell, were rigorously isolated. From the moment his daughter's " sicknes " appeared, the rector and his household were entirely cut off from the outside world. The churchyard was a mile away, far out of reach, and, imprisoned in his little domain, Robert Lenthall watched his nearest and dearest perish one by one until the death-roll totalled five, wondering every day when his own turn would come and who would be left to bury him in his kitchen-mead. The number seems the greater when we remember that, apart from this visitation, only two deaths were recorded in the wide parish of Hampden in that year—" Robert Hues a child " and " Jane Higly a mayd."

The general plan of the grounds has changed but little since Lenthall's day. The old kitchen garden, with a red brick wall to shelter it from the north, lies to the east of the house; as one follows the pathway through it to a little gate in the hedge, a round hollow on our left, from which the stagnant pond has now been drained, shows

Charles ... Bartlett f. 48

that this is the same track by which Robert Lenthall carried his dead to their graves. Through the gate a little orchard narrows to a point between a tall dark hedge of hollies and the garden boundary. This is the kitchen-mead. The trees are gnarled and twisted with age; some lean on many crutches; and the older branches of an ancient apple tree " by yᵉ hedgeside " seem roughly shaped in the likeness of a cross.

The Rectory looks a happy, peaceful spot to-day, with the sun pouring through its windows, as if no tragedy could ever have approached it. We follow the shady lane that leads from its western gate into a wider road bordered by a little group of comfortable farms, and, rounding the garden of a trim, thatched cottage to the left, we find ourselves on Hampden Common. We bear round the hedge to the right and follow the open ground through gorse and bracken for over half a mile. On our right a cottage here and there peeps out from among the orchards, and to the left, all the way, runs a great forest of beeches, broken at intervals by a group of larches or a spreading oak, while at times a giant ash encroaches in solitary state upon the fairway. Hampden Common may have no wide views like that at Nuffield, no breezy sense of open spaces like that of Cholesbury, but many a lover of the Chilterns would place it first upon his list. Its woodland paths are unsurpassed, and the glade along which we are walking changes direction from time to time to give us a series of different vistas each more attractive than the last. One such view Mr. Bathurst shows us in his picture, taken at the corner near the village school, looking across one of the little hollows that diversify our course. On the top of the opposite hill we turn into the straight which brings us by a broad stretch of turf to the road that runs over the ridge from Hampden House to Princes Risborough. In so far as the scattered village of Great Hampden can be said to have a centre, we may find it in this little group of cottages by the road, with the " Buckinghamshire Arms," which boasts the Earl of Buckinghamshire as its licensee, standing in the corner. Our walk now follows the road towards

Risborough; but this is a convenient spot from which we may diverge to visit the home and last resting-place of John Hampden the patriot.

Crossing the road by the inn, we follow the line of cottages that edge the common till we see, between two of them, a black gate with a footpath leading across the fields to the right. Taking this, we are soon descending the slope to Hampden House and the little church that sits beneath its wing, both half-hidden by trees. On our way we can borrow the church key at the thatched cottage that lies away to our left across the grass. Readers of guide-books soon become sceptical about mansions said to have belonged to families " from time immemorial," but it is sober truth in the case of Hampden House. Its present owner (the Earl of Buckinghamshire) can trace his descent from Hampdens who were lords of Hampden before the Conquest and nobody knows how long before that. Osbert of Hampden was dispossessed by a Norman invader, but became his steward, married his daughter and regained his former lordship, and from him the great John Hampden was directly descended in the male line. Here the family enjoyed every feudal privilege, including the right of " Gaol and Gallows " within their manor, were visited by their sovereigns, and intermarried with the principal families of the county.

The present house has suffered from many restorations, and only a projecting corner on the south side, known as King John's tower, is admitted by archæologists to be mediæval. The remainder is mostly eighteenth century. The whole of it was covered with cement in the reign of George III, and though parts of it have been stripped, showing a good red brick beneath, other parts are heavily plastered. Like many manor houses in the Chilterns it suggests solidity rather than beauty, and depends chiefly for its attraction upon its position and surroundings.

The little church, only separated from the manor house by a carriage drive, dates from the fourteenth century, but the walls of hard flint, rescued in modern times from a covering of plaster, fail to look their age, so well have they resisted the wear and tear of centuries. The Tudor woodwork in the roof of the porch, decorated with the five-petalled rose of York and Lancaster, appears more ancient to the inexpert eye. The interior has been much restored, but some of the old pews remain, carved with a variant of the linen-fold pattern by craftsmen who had seen the Wars of the Roses; their dimensions suggest that the worshippers of that day were less long in the leg than their descendants. But the visitor who has come on a Hampden pilgrimage will look in vain for any monument to the Patriot. A modern window has been put in to his memory; brasses to his ancestors, going back to the fifteenth century, and including his father and his grandfather, decorate the chancel wall. There is a particularly prominent monument to his descendant John, who died unmarried in 1754, erected by his cousin and successor, the Hon. Robert Trevor: within an oval frame above is an elaborate genealogical tree showing the descent of the Trevors from Ruth, eldest daughter of the greater John, with the battle of Chalgrove Field raging (in bas-relief) about its stem.[1] More attractive is the tablet erected by the great Hampden to his first wife Elizabeth. " The tender mother of an happy offspring, in nine hopeful children. In her pilgrimage the staie and comfort of her neighbours, the love and glory of a well-ordered family, the delight and happiness of tender parents, but a crown of blessings to a husband." But of the Hampden who upheld the Great Charter there is nothing. No stone marks his grave; and the entry of his burial on June 25, 1643, in the Parish Register was obviously an afterthought —squeezed in between the lines when the other entries of that year had already been written. This has caused some authorities to have serious doubts as to whether John Hampden was really brought home for burial. Lord Nugent gives a circumstantial account of the ceremony, based upon a contemporary news-sheet which he does not

[1] The Trevors became Viscounts Hampden, but their line failed with the death of the third viscount in 1820. The property then passed to the Hobarts, descended from the Patriot's youngest daughter, who added Hampden to their name and became Earls of Buckinghamshire.

quote verbatim.[1] But an extant letter written by one of Hampden's comrades in arms settles the question; it also seems to dispose of the rhetorical dying speech that has been attributed to the Patriot.   It was written by Colonel John Goodwin to his daughter, Lady Wharton of Upper Winchendon, on June 26, 1643: [2]

> " DEERE JENNY,
>   " I am now heere at Hampden in doinge the last duty for the deceased owner of it, of whome every honest man has a share in the losse, and therefore will do like-wise in the sorrowe. . . .   For all I can heere the last words he spake was to me, though he died six or 7 houres after I came away as in a slepe; truly Jenny (and I know you may easily be persuaded to it) he was a gallant man, an honest man, an able man; and, take all, I know nott to any man livinge second. . . .   I have writt to London for a black suite. I pray lett me begg of you a broad blacke Ribbon to hange about my standard. . . ."

Equally nameless is the grave of a remarkable old lady who was laid to rest in this churchyard twenty-one years later. The entry in the Register reads: " Elizabeth Hampden, wife of William Hampden, Esqr (L^d of Great Hamp-den) (she lived 90 years and a widdow 67 years and two months) was buried the 21st day of february 1664." Mother of John Hampden, the Patriot, aunt of Oliver Cromwell, the Lord Protector, she had lived to see the Restoration. What reminiscences she might have written!

We return to the " Buckinghamshire Arms," at the end of Great Hampden Common, and follow the road straight forward across a hollow. Hampden Woods still accompany us on the left. The trees were formerly neg-lected, but the skilful management of recent years has proved that good forestry need be no enemy to natural beauty. Those who love these woodland paths will avoid thrusting through the nurseries of young trees, designed

---

[1] *Some Memorials of John Hampden*, by Lord Nugent (1831).

[2] Printed by R. Gibbs in his *Buckinghamshire Miscellany*.

to preserve for future generations the sylvan charms that we enjoy to-day. Turning a corner we enter just such a clearing as early man might have carved from the forest to produce his daily bread. Here the road forks, and its two arms, with a cross-road further on, form a little triangle. We bear to the right, and, in passing the cross-road, note the solid bank on its further side. This is part of Grimsdyke, which we can trace along its most characteristic length from here to Lacey Green. The road enters the woods again and passes a few cottages on the right, known by the pleasant name of Green Hailey, and we soon reach a wood where it descends sharply. This is Kop Hill, which we must avoid on days of hill-climbing contests. We descend a few paces, and then climb the bank to the right where a footpath leads us forward through trees. The blue-grey mist that we see between their trunks suggests that we are on a promontory, but we are hardly prepared for the wonderful panorama that meets us when, at last, we step out into the open. The converging valleys of Thame and Thames lie before us, and, behind the Oxford hills, the long line of the Cotswolds is often visible. To our left Bledlow Ridge juts out across the Risborough gap, and beyond it the Berkshire Downs stretch away into Wiltshire, with White Horse Hill standing out above its fellows. The new railway line to Birmingham points straight to Brill Hill, which looks insignificant until you climb it and see its view, and thence the low ridge forming the northern edge of the vale of Aylesbury bounds the prospect to the east. A few steps down the hill to our left we find a curious excavation in the turf, laying bare the chalk below, that from here looks meaningless. This is the upper limb of Whiteleaf Cross, conspicuous to every traveller from the Oxford side. The cross, in fact, in itself measures eighty feet long, and its conical base descends the hill to the road at the bottom. Archæologists are at variance as to its origin. The Danes, of course, come into it: how many unlikely things have been laid to the charge of that industrious people, from neolithic dolmens to agricultural depression since the war! At the other

8

extreme comes a modern theory (which has won acceptance in unexpected quarters) that the cross was cut by Cavaliers of the royal garrison in Oxford to serve as a landmark in their Chiltern operations. But how were they allowed the leisure to cut it? Why did the Greencoats fail to obliterate it when they retired? And what use would it be? To-day it would, no doubt, make a useful ranging mark for a battery on Cuddesdon ridge; but, if Prince Rupert's troopers really required it to guide them through the obvious Risborough gap on their lightning raid to High Wycombe, how did they ever get home again unaided? Where doctors disagree, it is permissible for a layman to have his own theory: and to me it seems curious that the cross has not been more commonly connected with the village of Monks Risborough, which lies beneath us around its ancient church at the very foot of the steep descent. In the later days of monastic ownership the abbeys took little personal interest in their properties. But this manor was granted to monks of Canterbury long before the Norman Conquest, and it is surely not unlikely that at some time in the six centuries of their lordship it occurred to them to set their sacred symbol upon the hill above. I like to picture these old monks girding up their cassocks of an evening to climb the hill and devote their short leisure to this voluntary task, laying the chalk bare, foot by foot, to let their light shine before men over miles of open country. One difficulty, I admit, is the presence of a smaller but similar cross on the face of Bledlow Ridge across the valley; but neighbouring villages are jealous and imitative, and, when the cross of Whiteleaf won renown, Bledlow, with its equal opportunity, would not wish to lag behind.

From our point of vantage on the top, we can descend to the valley in any direction. A most attractive path to our right leads down through the beechwoods to the little inn below, whence we can visit the Kimbles and so to Wendover; or we can vary this route by retracing our steps to Green Hailey, and take a green lane to the left, on the near side of the first two cottages, that runs to Longdown farm, and, climbing again to the Missenden

road, leads to a path that runs through a corner of the Chequers estate to Great Kimble. But on so clear a day it is a pity to leave the summits; moreover, we should miss the Pink and Lily Inn, and men in London, to whom I have spoken of the view from Whiteleaf Cross, have asked me how it lies from the " Pink and Lily." Let us then repass Green Hailey, and, climbing a stile on the right, follow a path across a field into the beechwoods. When I last walked this way, I found a little outpost of the chair-leg-making industry in full swing right in the heart of the wood, where the trees had been felled. The mechanism was precisely the same as we have seen in the hut at Prestwood—the lathe and the swinging pole—but the shelter erected above them, just high enough in the centre for a man to stand upright, was full of interest. Two lines of straight poles leant together formed both walls and roof, tied together at the top by a horizontal pole to make the ridge and by lesser boughs at intervals down the sides. This simple structure was heavily thatched with twigs and seemed quite impervious to rain. In this way and in no other must the earliest dwellers in the Chilterns have made their homes in the days before history—before man had learned that flints can be bound together by a paste of burnt chalk, and that clay can be hardened into bricks by fire. Emerging from the trees, we follow the edge of the wood along an open down, and, where the wood ends, pass into the road on our left within a stone's throw of the " Pink and Lily."

The fame of this little inn rests neither upon its architectural charm nor its large accommodation. Substantial luncheons are spread on fine Sundays, and bread and cheese can be eaten on these summits at any time with a zest unknown to dwellers in the plain. But its name sticks in the mind as a meeting-place of so many memorable walks. He who starts from Princes Ris-borough Station below, here stops to take his first breath of genuine Chiltern air, while another who has followed the ascending scale of beauty from High Wycombe or Great Missenden pauses in reluctance to leave the heights. Its very remoteness from the world of affairs and post-war problems lifts a burden from our shoulders and we take the road again with lightened hearts. We like it all the better because it was a favourite with Rupert Brooke, " dead ere his prime " and laid to rest in distant Mudros. Brooke was a genuine lover of the Chilterns, and Mr. Marsh, in his very attractive memoir, records how tramping here one day with his friend, Jacques Raverat, he burst into one of those spontaneous jingles with which he was wont to celebrate the inns that pleased him. The third and fourth lines were supplied by his more critical companion:

> " Never came there to the Pink
> Two such men as we, I think,
> [Never came there to the Lily
> Two men quite so richly silly,]
> So broad, so supple, and so tall,
> So modest and so brave withal,
> With hearts so clear, such noble eyes,
> Filled with such sage philosophies,
> Thirsty for Good, secure of Truth,
> Fired by a purer flame than youth,
> Serene as age, but not so dirty,
> Old, young, mature, being under thirty.
> Were ever two so fierce and strong,
> Who drank so deep, and laughed so long,
> So proudly meek, so humbly proud,
> Who walked so far, and sang so loud ? " [1]

That is the spirit in which we leave the " Pink and Lily " and choose our homeward way. The inn stands where three roads meet—from Great Hampden, from Princes Risborough, from Lacey Green. There is also a green lane close beside it which makes a pleasant walk to Speen. This lane crosses the Grims Dyke at a cottage called Coppice House, half a mile away; if we there take the sunken footpath to the right, we are walking in its ditch, and can follow it along its most interesting portion as far as Lacey Green. But for once we prefer the high road running straight to that village; for all the way it keeps close to the edge of the escarpment, and from it we

[1] Quoted by courtesy of the literary executors and of Messrs. Sidgwick & Jackson, publishers of *Rupert Brooke : a Memoir*, by Edward Marsh.

can see the long line of Bledlow Ridge running up to its culminating point in Wain Hill, the buttress of the downs that stretch unbroken to the Thames. As we look back, a fine stretch of country is framed by the gap, with the graceful outlines of Wheatley and Shotover Hills behind. These we may trust to remain unspoilt, for they lie within the orbit of Oxford, and a distinguished body of great and learned men of Town and Gown is pledged to preserve the summits round the city from disfigurement. Nor, till now, have we anything on this Chiltern ridge that we need be ashamed to show to Oxford. The " Pink and Lily " hides behind a group of trees, and so does Widmer Farm. The hamlet of Loosley Row lies below the horizon, and the Whip Inn at the top crouches inconspicuously beside the fine old windmill—the only work of man that can sit upon these rounded hilltops as if it grew there. The space between the road and the edge is narrow, but it might support a row of bungalows, and a too familiar notice-board excites our worst fears. It contains the usual offer of building plots for sale on the " Widmer Hill Building Estate ": freehold sites, water laid on, and all the rest of it. But at the bottom we read, with something of a shock—" Apply The Bursar, Merton College, Oxford." It almost makes one wish one had gone to Cambridge.

And now we must be getting home. Somewhere we must descend the inner rim into the little valley on our left; we can pass through Lacey Green and then go down by the footpath to Speen; or we can keep along the hill to Walter's Ash (where a road on our right leads to Bradenham), passing Grimsdyke House, long the home of Sir W. S. Gilbert, the Savoyard; and eventually take a turn to the left which brings us into the middle of Upper North Dean. Descending any of these curving valleys we reach the bottom of Cryers Hill, within sight of the Hughenden Woods, where a motor-bus will take us swiftly to High Wycombe or back to Great Missenden.

CHAPTER IX

ROUND ABOUT ASHRIDGE

IT is difficult to set a definite limit to our Penn Country. It is a question of quality rather than of frontiers, and the decision as to where this quality ends is largely a matter of individual sensibility. No hard and fast line could meet with general acceptance, but, as one moves eastward, there is, to me, a distinct feeling of something different when one comes to the valley of the Bulbourne. It is not a question of beauty or interest. The upper waters of the Gade are delightful, but their quiet charm is that of the Colne or the Lea; and if we push over the breezy ridges to do homage to Bacon at Gorhambury or to Charles Lamb at Mackerye End by Wheathampstead, we can go forward to the other end of Hertfordshire without noting any definite change in the character of the scenery. But it becomes obviously different from the typical Penn Country. The gap that runs from Watford to Tring, beginning with the Gade and Bulbourne valleys and having royal Berkhampstead for its capital and centre, has always been a great dividing line. Through it the Romans drove their Akeman Street to Aylesbury and Bicester; and the Great Junction Canal, which made a great detour to the west to avoid the gentle eminences of northern London, negotiated its easy gradients without difficulty. The main line of the London and North Western Railway followed on their tracks—the first to cross the Chilterns—and gradually changed the character of the valley. But even here there is an exception. At the northern end of the pass the hills increase on either side. Facing the heights of Wigginton there rises on the eastern ridge a great bluff crowned by Ashridge Park and Berkhampstead Common, which may surely claim close kinship with the woods and commons of Great Hampden and must be added to our bag. A great portion of this country has already been secured for the nation through a timely appeal by the National Trust. It has thus been saved from bricks and mortar; and, when the exuberance of new possession wears off and the grateful public ceases to strew the woods and commons with picnic litter, it should form a very valuable addition to the patches of old English country that are being preserved for future generations.

Tring Station lies nearly two miles from the centre of Tring and a mile and a half from the main road from Berkhampstead. But it is a convenient starting-place for our eastern ridge. We take the lane to Aldbury running in open fields over the shoulder of Pitstone Hill, which lies at the mouth of the pass like an island in a river delta; and we soon see the white church tower and lichen-covered roofs of the village below us. The centre of Aldbury, where the roads meet, has been painted by many artists: the pond in the centre, with elms on one side and the old stocks upon the other, and a dream of a half-timbered house behind, makes a very pleasant picture. The church, which stands back on the slope of the hill, has been much restored. The Verney chapel in the south aisle has, in its centre, an altar tomb with fine recumbent effigies of Sir Robert Whittingham, who was killed in the Wars of the Roses, and his wife; it is said to have been removed here from the old religious house at Ashridge at the time of the Dissolution. On the wall above them are the very " animated busts " of Sir Richard Anderson and Lady Elizabeth his wife, he in his full-bottomed wig and she with her curls intricately coiled, after the fashion of the days of William and Mary; they lived at Pendley Manor, between here and Tring, and passed it on to the family of Simon Harcourt, who married their only surviving daughter.

The escarpment of the Chilterns rises steep and high behind Aldbury village, and a sloping path runs up to its summit on Moneybury Hill. Here a long avenue from Ashridge Park comes through to the edge, and the

top of the column erected in memory of the third Duke
of Bridgewater stands out above the trees.   But we will
go forward four miles to Ivinghoe Beacon before ascending, and return through the wilder beauties of Ivinghoe
Common to Ashridge.   At the end of the village we pass
on the left the grounds of Stocks, a property left by
will to Sir Edward Grey (now Lord Grey of Fallodon)
and sold by him in 1891 to Mr. Humphry Ward.   Here
Mrs. Humphry Ward wrote many of her novels: Aldbury
can easily be recognized as the " Clinton Magna " of
The Story of Bessie Costrell and there are good Chiltern
walks in *Marcella*.   A hundred years before the house
belonged to James Adam Gordon, a close friend of Sir
Walter Scott, and it was through this connexion that
Sir Walter heard the name of the neighbouring village
which suggested to him a title for *Ivanhoe*.

Passing from behind Pitstone Hill we see the bare downs
stretching before us, ending in the rounded point of
Ivinghoe Beacon.   Mr. Bathurst has drawn it from the
slopes of Pitstone Hill.   Ivinghoe itself lies below us on
the left: it is a picturesque old village, looking particularly well as one ascends from the vale to the foothill on
which it stands, but we continue along the road that
follows the ancient line of the Icknield Way till we reach
the little wood below the Beacon.   We leave the road to
ascend it.   Arriving at the top we expect to find a solid
ridge of downland stretching away behind: actually we
stand on a projecting peninsula, united to the Ashridge
massif by a narrow isthmus.   Behind is a great rounded
hollow, not unlike the crater of a volcano that has burst
its bounds towards the vale, with the long straight line of
Dunstable Downs continuing the wall on the further side.
The view is magnificent.   It perhaps lacks incident; we
cannot pick out points like Wheatley Hill or Wittenham
Clumps or White Horse Hill, or follow the wanderings
of Thame and Thames, as we can from the Chiltern
escarpment further west.   But nowhere do we get so
clearly a sense of illimitable distance.   The low wooded
ridges of Woburn are but a wrinkle on the great plain of
rich agricultural land watered by the Ouzel and the Ivel,

Charles H Bathurst 1928

IVINGHOE BEACON.

and we look past them into the heart of England.
Rupert Brooke knew this escarpment from end to end,
but it must have been somewhere hereabouts—Ivinghoe
Beacon or Aston Clinton Hill—that he conceived his poem
named *The Chilterns*:

> " I shall desire and I shall find
> The best of my desires :
> The autumn road, the mellow wind
> That soothes the darkening shires,
> And laughter and inn fires.

> " White mist above the black hedgerows,
> The slumbering Midland plain,
> The silence where the clover grows,
> And the dead leaves in the lane,
> Certainly these remain . . ." [1]

We turn back along our narrow spur and, in the dip
before we reach the main ridge, pick up the open road
that runs across Ivinghoe Downs to Little Gaddesden.   It
is a good road all the way, and these downlands and the
commons beyond through which we pass are all protected by the National Trust.   We climb Steps Hill and,
soon reaching our highest elevation—something over 800
feet—we enjoy a fine view on our left looking back to
Ivinghoe Beacon.   On Dunstable Downs across the hollow
the National Trust has purchased more land at Whipsnade,
which is being converted into an open-air zoological park
where animals can enjoy a greater freedom than in
Regent's Park.   It is an interesting experiment, and the
only criticism has come from certain misanthropic
country-lovers who suggest that this barrage of wild
beasts should have been laid right across the Chilterns
nearer London.   Passing a long common of gorse and
bracken we soon come to the palings of Ashridge Park.
A road to the right descends to the valley at Northchurch,
and that on the left follows the park boundary to Little
Gaddesden.

The present house at Ashridge was erected about the
year 1810 and is an elaborate Gothic building designed

[1] Printed by permission of the literary executors and of Messrs.
Sidgwick & Jackson, publishers of the *Complete Poems* of Rupert
Brooke.

by Wyatt and finished by his nephew, which seems to take less kindly to its environment of beechwoods than the simpler structures of Penn House or The Vache or Crowsley; but the history of the site takes us back to ages far more remote, when Edmond, Earl of Cornwall, nephew of King Henry III, founded here a monastery for monks of the Order of Bons Hommes, which he had introduced into England from the Continent. To their charge he entrusted a very sacred relic he had purchased in Hanover, alleged to be no less than a drop of the blood of Christ contained in a golden casket. Many pilgrims came with gifts to see it, but after the Dissolution it was taken to London for examination and pronounced to be " honey clarified and coloured with saffron." Nor was this the only relic Earl Edmond gave to Ashridge. After the unpleasant custom of his day by his last will and testament he bequeathed his own heart to Ashridge and his bones to the abbey of Hales. The poet Skelton, tutor to the young Henry VIII, describes in his *Garlande of Laurell* a visit to

> " The bone homes of Ashridge beside Barcamstede
> Where the sange royall is, Christis blode so rede,"

and decides that " a pleasanter place than Ashridge is, harde were to finde." When the monks and their relics had been ejected, Edward VI gave it to his sister the Princess Elizabeth, who lived here peaceably for ten years till, on the outbreak of Wyat's rebellion, her half-sister Queen Mary ordered her arrest. Ill though she was, Elizabeth was forced to leave her bed and was carried to the Tower in a litter.

A new house was built in 1606 by Lord Chancellor Ellesmere, and it remained in the Egerton family for many generations. His descendants were remarkable for their great alliances and acquired many titles. His son John became first Earl of Bridgewater: he married the Earl of Derby's daughter, and, as " Lord President of Wales," produced Milton's masque of *Comus*, with music by Lawes, at a great entertainment given by him at Ludlow Castle in 1637, three of his own children taking part.

His son and grandson both married daughters of dukes, and his great-grandson Scroop Egerton, who married in succession daughters of the great Duke of Marlborough and of the Duke of Bedford, was himself created first Duke of Bridgewater. It was in honour of his younger son Francis, the third Duke, that the great granite column was erected with the blue-green copper ball on top, which we have viewed from Aldbury: it is seen from the house at the end of an avenue, a mile and a half in length, called Prince's Riding, and is inscribed to the memory of " the Father of Inland Navigation." This remarkable man succeeded his brother at the age of twelve, and at a very early age became interested in water transport. He owned coal-mines at Worsley in Lancashire and conceived the idea that he might effect great saving by constructing canals connecting his collieries with Manchester. He was fortunate in enlisting the services of Brindley, the celebrated engineer, and the canals were successfully completed. He then obtained authority to construct a more difficult canal between Liverpool and Manchester. All these works had been finished before the Duke had passed his thirty-sixth year. The expense had been enormous and at times brought the rich Duke almost to the verge of bankruptcy: for long he kept his personal expenditure down to £400 a year. But his judgment proved sound, and at the age of forty he was in possession of a princely income from his undertakings. He subscribed £100,000 to the Loyalty Loan without inconvenience. In his youth he had fallen in love with the beautiful Duchess of Hamilton, and after her marriage to another he became a confirmed misogynist and would have no woman of any kind in his house. His dukedom died with him in 1803: the earldom passed to his cousin John William Egerton, son of the Bishop of Durham, who became seventh earl; but over his canals in Lancashire he determined to maintain his control as long as possible. The law of England limits the settlement of estates to the lifetime of living persons and twenty-one years after. The duke settled his property for the lifetime of all peers who took their seats in the House of Lords before his death and their issue then living, and also of a number of his relations and friends with their children. One of the commoners survived till 1883, so that the trust continued for more than one hundred years. His cousin and heir, the seventh Earl of Bridgewater, also left an eccentric will, which became the subject of a *cause célèbre*. The story is told by Sir Bernard Burke in his *Vicissitudes of Noble Families*. Having no children, he bequeathed his great property first to his widow, next to his brother Francis, and then to his great-nephew, Lord Alford, heir to the Earl of Brownlow, on the following condition: " If the said Lord Alford should die without having attained the rank of Marquis or Duke, or should not have attained either of those dignities within five years after he had become Lord Brownlow, the property was to go to his brother, the Hon. Charles Henry Cust, subject to the like term." The testator died in 1823. His brother Francis, who succeeded him as eighth (and last) Earl of Bridgewater, died in 1829. The testator's widow lived till 1849, when the condition became operative. Lord Alford succeeded to the property, but died in 1851 leaving a young son. He had not become Duke or Marquis and died just too soon to become Earl of Brownlow. " Then arose the point, ' Was his brother or his son entitled to the estate? ' On the one side it was urged that the late possessor being dead, without having obtained the stipulated grade, his descendants had thereby incurred the penalty of forfeiture. To this it was replied, that only one year having expired, the matter must as yet be considered doubtful. Both parties appealed to law, and law in its court of highest appeal—the House of Lords—decided that the condition, being contrary to the principles of the English constitution, and one which the devisee had no legitimate means of controlling, should be passed over, and the will read without it." Ashridge thus passed to the youthful Earl of Brownlow.

Outside the eastern gate of the Park the village of Little Gaddesden straggles pleasantly along the road. There is a comfortable inn, the Bridgewater Arms, and there are many good cottages with flowers in the gardens.

By the park gate is a well-designed stone seat facing a fountain surmounted by a cross, erected by the villagers in memory of a notable benefactress, Lady Marion Alford. She was widow of the Lord Alford whose failure to become a marquis caused so much ado, and looked after the welfare of the estate during the youth and subsequent illnesses of her invalid son.   She founded the Bede Houses for poor widows of the parish, and was a generous contributor to the restoration of the church.   Lord Beaconsfield, visiting at Ashridge with his wife, thought her " a woman of commanding ability."

The church, which stands by itself in the fields behind the village, has a curious interest.   One is accustomed to find in other churches scattered examples of the extravagant praises with which the eighteenth century was wont to adorn the memorials of the great; but nowhere is such flattery so insistent as in this little church crowded on every side with tombs of impossibly perfect Egertons. Never were epitaphs longer or more fulsome, or family pride more completely satisfied.   Take that of John Egerton, who died in 1700,—" Earl of Bridgewater, Viscount Brackley, Baron of Ellesmere, Knight of the Honble Order of the Bath, One of the Governors of the Charterhouse, One of the Lord Justices of England, First Lord Commissioner of ye Admiralty, Lord Lieutenant of the County of Bucks, and One of the Lords of the most hon^{ble} Privy Council to his Majesty King William ye III. . . ."   A long chapter follows attributing to him every known virtue, and then—" This monument can no more contain his full and just character than this marble will outlast his memory."   And so on all round the walls, the high-born wives receiving even fuller meed of praise than their husbands.   It is noteworthy that the only two members of the family whose names are generally remembered to-day receive the shortest notices.   Of the " Father of Inland Navigation," it is simply said: " He will ever be memorable among ' those who were honoured in their generations and were the glory of their times.' *Impulit ille rates ubi duxit aratra colonus.*" [1]   Francis,

---

[1] " He drove his boats where farmers drove their ploughs."

the last earl, certainly has an allegorical group in which a dolphin, a stork and an elephant figure with a lady reading a book, but the text is simple: " He bequeathed £8000 as a reward to literary men for writing essays to prove the benevolence of God as displayed in the works of the Creation." This bequest produced the famous Bridgewater Treatises, contributed by eight chosen writers. He also left to the British Museum the valuable Egerton MSS. of French and Italian literature and a sum of £12,000. He was a Fellow of All Souls and a Prebend of Durham, and undeniably an eccentric: he spent much of his time in Paris, and the French police reported that his house there was filled with dogs and cats dressed up like ladies and gentlemen, which he took out for drives in his carriage and fed at his own table.

Amid the vast slabs of marble lauding forgotten Egertons it is a pleasure to find a few small tablets squeezed in to prove that lesser mortals were sometimes buried there. One of them is a testimonial to Little Gaddesden. It used to be said that anyone who bought a property in Hertfordshire had to pay so many years' purchase for the good air. A " lady from Yorkshire " named Ann Norton would have thought it just. " In search of health," says her tablet, " she accidentally passed a few days in this parish, and having found benefit from its pure air, fixed her residence here, where she expired on the 13th day of April 1796 in the 73rd year of her age, and was by her particular desire interred in the adjoining Church-yard." But there was another resident of Little Gaddesden to whom I turn my mind still more readily from the surfeit of panegyric. While the Egertons were piling title on title, there was living here a farmer named William Ellis, who set down upon paper his theory of all kinds of husbandry and published it in 1733 by the title of *Chiltern and Vale Farming Explained*. Mr. G. Eland, whose intimate researches into old local industries make such good reading,[1] asserts that Ellis's own farming was not a success; but his teaching on

[1] *Old Works and Old Days*, and *The Chilterns and the Vale*, by G. Eland.

many points seems to have been in advance of his age. At any rate he was clearly just the kind of farmer that one likes to meet and walk with for a mile along the road, for I am sure he talked exactly as he wrote. Much of his book is somewhat technical for general quotation, but, as a good sample of his breezy style, read what he had to say about

" The Nature and Improvement of the White ELDER."

" This I believe I may venture to say, is a new Chapter in Print, . . . as being not wrote of in this distinct and ample Manner, by any Author before my self, as I know of; tho' in my humble Opinion, they deserve the Preference to several others that have been more enlarged on, whose Uses and Values are far short of these excellent Trees: The first of the white Elder was introduced into these Parts, by the late curious *Simon Hartcourt,* Esq; of *Penly,* from whom I had many Cuttings that now grow in my Garden-hedge to a great Height, and to an East and West Aspect, by which it enjoys the Rising and the Setting of the Sun, that is more than ordinary necessary to the due Maturation of this Berry; because if they are not full ripe when gathered, their Liquor will be spoiled: as, I understand, a Hogshead or two of their Wine was by injudicious hands; who seeing the Berries ripe on one Side did not examine whether the other was so too; which caused them being gathered too soon, and their Wine eager in a little time: Whereas if this Berry is gathered in a dry time and full ripe, it has made Wine, that has deceived a Gentleman I was in Company with, of great Judgment in many other Liquors; who took it for *French* Frontigniac, which it comes very near to, both in Taste and Colour: But this cannot be done without a particular Ingredient that I had an Account of from Mr. *Carbury* the late Minister's Widow of *Ivinghoe,* who was the most famous for this sort of Oeconomy of any in this Country; and which with several different Receipts, among other serviceable Secrets, never yet Printed, I intend, God willing, to publish as soon as I well can, if I am encourag'd thereto by such as are wellwishers to the good of their country."

From Little Gaddesden we step straight into Ashridge Park and, following the sloping drive to the left, soon come within sight of the mansion. The whole park is at present in a state of flux. An army of workmen is busy upon the house, which has been purchased and given to the Conservative party by Mr. Urban Broughton. It has already been stripped of the many treasures it contained: the famous sixteenth-century stained glass windows, imported from the ancient abbey of Steinfeld in Germany and re-erected here early in the last century, were sold at Sotheby's for £27,000 and have happily found a resting-place in the South Kensington Museum. But it still retains the trees—beech and chestnut, lime and ash, —which have always been its chief glory. A great portion of the park, and all Berkhampstead Common, which runs in a narrow strip along its western side and widens out towards Berkhampstead, have been secured by the National Trust: and the edge of the hill above Aldbury, including the Bridgewater Column, has been purchased by the owner of Stocks for the benefit of that village. Here and there barbed wire fences check the rambler, but other negotiations are in progress, and, as a net result, a very extensive stretch of fine country will be preserved for the enjoyment of the public. May the public prove worthy of the gift.

Passing across the front of the house we find a road running to the left among fine beeches, which soon descends a hollow to the park gate, which admits us to Berkhampstead Common. On our right rises the famous group of mighty trees called Frithesden Beeches. From here we can either keep to the road or take any one of the paths running forward across the common. It is a good open common with plenty of sun and air, and little picturesque groups of pine trees rise here and there to give it character. Crossing the golf links we come to the ridge above the road which descends by the ancient mound of Berkhampstead Castle, and sit on the brow to consider the situation. Below us lies the town of Berkhampstead, the chief place of the curiously shaped Hundred of Dacorum, which in early days was always a royal appanage. The place is full of mediæval history: in later times the poet Cowper was born at its Rectory, and its time-honoured school never prospered more than now. Here and there among its modernized streets one finds a gem of a seventeenth-century, half-timbered house. But we have not come to walk in towns. We lift up our eyes to the long low ridge behind, sloping upwards from left to right, and plan a course to lead us back towards the centre of the Penn Country.

The obvious route is too impossibly obvious. Straight up the opposite slope runs the main road from Berkhampstead to Chesham. It is the only main road that crosses the ridge between Bulbourne and Chess and it is amply sufficient to carry all the cross traffic, which is as it should be. The early portion is attractive. The grounds of Ashlyns, the new home of the Foundling Hospital, transferred from Bloomsbury, crown the first ridge, and beyond the deep ravine of Hookeridge Bottom is an interesting village called Ashley Green. But after this the road has its *longueurs*. If we want to go to Chesham we ought not to miss the glorious open stretch of gorse on Ley Hill Common, which lies to the left. But do we want to go to Chesham? Like all the old Chiltern towns, a part of it is good. The group formed by the old church and The Bury, the home of successive squires of the Lowndes family for many a generation, makes a charming picture with all the attractions of wood, hill and water. But this lies upon the further side, and the ribbon development of the town up every valley makes the approach uninteresting. The rambler in search of open country must surely pass to north or south. Shall we take the hills and wide horizons of the north, or wander among the maze of lanes and hidden villages that lie towards Chorleywood and Rickmansworth? Each route has its own particular beauties and is well worth following. Let us first strike

9

straight across the northern uplands, and then return to enjoy a day of little things—little lanes, little hollows, little villages—as we ramble by devious tracks from Box-moor to descend at evening to the lower waters of the Chess.

CHAPTER X

NORTHCHURCH TO WENDOVER

THE broad main street of Berkhampstead follows the old Roman road that once rang to the tramp of the legions and is still adequate to-day to carry a great volume of motor traffic to and from the Midlands. It is the obvious and only route for all wheeled transport up and down the valley, but to a walker the tow-path of the Grand Junction Canal offers superior attractions. It is very different from the severely commercial canals one finds in industrial districts, and in parts is far more like a river. It is already acquiring a pleasantly old-fashioned look. Its gaily-painted barges ride bravely on its waters and the white semi-circular bridges cast perfect reflections in the placid surface underneath. One is neither splashed with mud nor smothered with dust, and, if one is careful to avoid walking between the barge and the horse that tows it, there is little or no danger to a pedestrian. The tow-path let it be: we start up the valley with the canal upon our right, and the infant stream of the Bulbourne, hiding at times beneath a bed of watercress, keeping close company upon the left. If the Father of Inland Navigation still, in spirit, revisits Ashridge hill, he would have every cause to gaze with satisfaction on the valley below. Road and rail may offer advantages to the slaves of time, but surely, for men of wealth and leisure, one of these roomy barges on the canal is the high-water mark of luxury in travel. Smooth and noiseless running; no punctures or police-traps; a comfortable chair on deck or a cosy corner in the cabin. When the virtues of peacefulness and contemplation are given again their proper place in a useful life, society will come to town, not by

Rolls-Royce or London, Midland and Scottish, but by Grand Junction.

A mile and a half from Great Berkhampstead we see across the field to the left the old tower of Northchurch, formerly known as Berkhampstead St. Mary. It is an interesting old church with a very picturesque churchyard. By a venerable yew tree, in a corner facing the main road, stands the old Rectory, one of the most attractive black-and-white houses in the district. The church itself has been much restored, and the short substantial tower, and the arches within which sustain it, alone give any great sense of its undoubted antiquity. But the whole has great beauty, and some of the windows are noticeably good. A brass on the south wall in memory of " Peter the Wild Boy," with his portrait (after Bartolozzi) engraved above, records a curious incident of the early eighteenth century, when the awakening of scientific interest led to many odd experiments. The gist of the story is told on the tablet. A black-haired boy, nearly naked, with skin tanned by the weather, " was found Wild in the Forest of Hertswold near Hanover in the year 1725: he then appeared to be about 12 years old. In the following year he was brought to England by the order of the Late Queen Caroline and the ablest Masters were provided for him. But proving incapable of speaking or of receiving any instruction, a comfortable provision was made for him by Her Majesty at a farm house in this parish where he continued till the end of his inoffensive life." He died in 1785 at the estimated age of seventy-two. It is difficult to-day to understand the stir made by this poor idiot in the polite world. There are constant references to him in contemporary writings: Archdeacon Paley quoted the case to illustrate a point in his *Moral and Political Philosophy*. He spent most of his life at Broadway Farm on the other side of Berkhampstead, and the collar which he wore, directing anyone who found him straying to return him to that farm, was formerly kept at Ashridge Park. An early historian of the county adds a few further details: " It is reported that his countenance much resembled that of Socrates.

Charles J. Bathurst. 1928

He could never be taught to articulate any word, though he hummed a tune or two. He was very fond of ale and tobacco, and had retained so much of his Court breeding as to kiss the hand of the person who gave him money." There is no indication that the writer meant to be cynical.

We continue along the canal bank, looking back to enjoy the view which Mr. Bathurst has drawn from the far side of the water. At the next bridge we take the road to the left, through the picturesque hamlet of Dudswell, and crossing Akeman Street find a lane opposite that soon becomes a footpath. A great spur of the Chilterns, pushing out into the valley, lies before us, and at its foot we come to a spot where six lanes and footpaths meet. Any way up the hill leads to the village of Wigginton which lies on the top: the pleasantest route is by the footpath which ascends through a wood of pine trees. The village itself has little to detain us: its common has been enclosed, its church rebuilt, and many new cottages have been lately erected without care for æsthetic considerations. But the steep climb is more than rewarded by the glorious prospect. Most of the great Chiltern views look outwards away from London over the open spaces to the north and west; and, so far as I have seen them, there is no inward view to compare with this from Wigginton. From Coleshill or from Penn, from Fawley or from Turville Park, the interest lies in the distance, in places far outside the hills themselves. But Wigginton seems to have been placed just so in order to reveal the loveliness of a Chiltern valley. Opposite rises the ridge above Aldbury with the Bridgewater Monument rising among the trees and the gorse of Berkhampstead Common gilding the brow above the vale till the thin smoke of the town screens the hill. On our own side a deep ravine lies below us and, beyond, the woods of Champneys; the slopes, that looked so flat as we followed the canal up the bottom, are seen from here to be a succession of spurs, each crowned with trees, continued down to the widening of the valley, where the Gade, flowing from the eastern hills, carries the Bulbourne with it round the corner behind the high clump of firs near Westbrook Hay. Many lanes meet at Wigginton. One runs to Tring Station, another to North-church, and two run over the hill by Tring Park, one of them aptly named "The Twist." But our way lies to Cholesbury, and we can take the main road without mis-givings, for the desperate hills behind preserve us from any press of traffic. We leave Wigginton through an avenue of oaks, following the road that leads southwards to Chesham; and in half a mile see a path running straight across the fields to our right, with an intermittent bank beside it. This marks the line of the ancient earthwork called Grims Ditch or Dyke, which we encounter so continually as we ramble on these Chiltern summits. It always runs somewhere near the watershed; but, where the watershed comes just above the escarpment, it retires a little to leave a stretch of upland between the ditch and the edge. At almost any point one can cross it without noticing it; but, if one definitely sets out to walk along it, starting with a stretch where bank and ditch are clearly visible, one can follow it for many miles without great difficulty. In some places it has been obliterated by the plough; but even here, when one has become used to the look of it, one can often pick out a bit of the bank in a field-boundary, or find the ditch in a sunken footpath. Of the parts I know, the best-preserved is that running from Great Hampden woods past the village of Lacey Green. Its pursuit makes an interesting paper-chase, and only so can one form any sound idea as to its origin and purpose. Many and many a ream of paper has been spent by antiquaries upon this problem. Some class it as a de-fensive earthwork—an early trench-line—while others stamp it as an ancient boundary between the Saxon king-doms of Mercia and Wessex. Many have attributed it to King Offa, who had a palace at Benson, because he made a somewhat similar earthwork on the marches of Wales. There is a dyke running from Benson to Henley, between Nettlebed and Stoke Row, that might more probably have been his work; it is sometimes called Grims Dyke, but it obviously has no connection with this other.[1] Parts of

[1] The tendency to apply the name of Grims Dyke to any straight line of earthworks in the Chilterns has led to much confusion.

our Grims Dyke may at one time or another have served
these purposes. Warriors may have used some length of
it for cover; but as one walks along it one notes that sometimes it gives a field of fire on one side, sometimes on the
other, and more often sedulously avoids a near strategic
point. Nor, if we take it as a whole, does it mark the
boundary of any kingdom known to history. If we follow
it with an open mind two facts emerge. Ditch and trench
are obviously very old—older than any farm about their
course—and, if they form a boundary, they allot a good
stretch of upland pasturage to the people of the Vale.
Surely in an annual strife for summer pastures all war
began, and the need for boundaries first arose: a need
already felt in the days when Abraham and Lot trekked
from Haran into Canaan.

" And Abram was very rich in cattle, in silver, and in
gold. . . . And Lot also, which went with Abram, had
flocks and herds and tents. And the land was not able
to bear them, that they might dwell together: for their
substance was great, so that they could not dwell together.
" And there was a strife between the herdmen of
Abram's cattle and the herdmen of Lot's cattle: and the
Canaanite and the Perizzite dwelled then in the land.
And Abram said unto Lot, Let there be no strife, I pray
thee, between me and thee, and between my herdmen and
thy herdmen; for we be brethren. . . ."

Such things must have occurred in every primitive pas-
toral community. Here, when the harvest was in and
the winter storms began, the live-stock was gathered in
the fields near the villages: and, when spring returned and
the time came to till the lower ground, the herdmen of
the sheltered " denes " in the hills—Gaddesden or Hampden, Missenden or Hambleden—would drive the flocks
and herds of their villages back to the upland pastures,
and there they would meet other herdmen coming up the
other side from the Great Vale. If they found no room for
all, they would fight, while the brigand outlaws lurking
in the thickets—the Chiltern Canaanites and Perizzites—

helped themselves to all the meat they wanted. In course of time the lords of the hills and the lords of the cities of the plain would come together and agree to erect a visible boundary for their mutual advantage and force their herdmen to respect it. Thus a continuous line would eventually be laid between the Chiltern denes and the Vale below. This may seem a fanciful suggestion, but it fits the facts. Grims Dyke would make a very equitable division for such a purpose, but is singularly ill-sited for the boundary of a warlike kingdom. It is interesting to note, by the way, that in the remoter Chilterns the word " cattle " retains the old meaning that it had for the translators of the Authorized Version of the Bible: farmers still speak of " cow-cattle," to distinguish them from other cattle such as sheep or swine.

Grims Dyke can be explored by starting from almost any point in the upper Chilterns, but for to-day we will leave it and make for Cholesbury. Continuing along this attractive stretch of road and passing the woods of Champneys with bracken straying through the fences on both sides, we come to a dividing of the ways and bear to the right. Between the two roads lie the open Flats, sloping gently to a hollow, and, beyond, a long ridge of common gay with gorse, and an old windmill waving its sails against the sky. In the corner of the common, to our right, is the village of Cholesbury, with grass running up to the cottage doors and high trees behind it; at the other end, on the tip of the spur, is Hawridge, and the county boundary runs along the whole length of the common. The windmill between them (which belongs to Hawridge) at one time threatened to fall into decay, like so many of its fellows; but it found a guardian angel in Miss Doris Keane, the talented actress who thrilled us all in *Romance* and has her country home in the village; and it now stands up to the wind as stoutly as ever.

Cholesbury is an attractive village with many fine old farm-houses about it. The wide open common gives it a spacious, airy feeling that is particularly noticeable when one comes the other way by the close shaded lanes from The Lee or Wendover and suddenly steps out into the open. But the view of church and village from the common is less enjoyable since the War, for a new bungalow of the most unfortunate variety has been planted at the most conspicuous point, right in the centre of the picture. Choose our standpoint where we may, we cannot avoid it. By way of contrast, the most interesting thing in Cholesbury is so retiring that you would never notice it unless you went to look for it. This is a great oval earthwork planted with trees, which encloses an area nearly 300 yards long and about 200 yards wide. It includes in its perimeter two ponds and also the church; but the ground has been levelled in the churchyard where the trench must originally have bordered the main road. It is marked on the map as " Danish camp." To early antiquaries anything rounded was Danish, anything square Roman; but experts have pointed out that it closely resembles the description given by the historian Tacitus of the British towns as they were found by the Romans. Its size suggests that it was an important place, and a lesser earthwork found near Hawridge may have been an advanced fort pushed out as a defence against invaders coming up the Chess valley.

There are good walks from Cholesbury to north or south of the line we are taking to-day. The first time I came to tramp in these parts I was strolling peacefully through High Scrubs, when a great kangaroo sprang out of a thicket and hopped across my path. I can promise you no such excitement to-day; since food ran short in the War, strange animals no longer enjoy the beauties of Tring Park and escape to lend an Antipodean touch to the woods round Cholesbury. But there is still a very good walk past Scrubs Wood to Hastoe whence a delightful footpath leads down to the Vale at Tring. To the south is a stretch of broken country where the Chess valley ends in many smaller valleys radiating fanlike from the town of Chesham. Each tributary dale is divided from its neighbour by a sharp " ridge "—Hawridge, Asheridge, Chartridge, Hundridge and the like—and the whole district is remarkable for the unspoilt beauty of its old homesteads.

The next point on our road is the hamlet of St. Leonards, a quiet little spot where many ways meet. Hence a road runs north along a promontory to Aston Hill; it attains a height of over 850 feet—the loftiest part of the Chilterns—and gives views of extraordinary extent before it curls down the steep hill to Aston Clinton. It is probably the finest northward prospect from the Chiltern escarpment that is open to the motorist sitting in his car. But as a walking route to Wendover it has the disadvantage of ending in two and a half miles of busy road bordering Halton Camp. To-day, at any rate, we will keep to the upland lanes a little longer.

The little church that gives its name to St. Leonards is quaint and interesting. Its list of known vicars goes back to 1273 and it was long a cell served by the monks of Missenden Abbey. Its walls are of great antiquity; but it lost its roof and fell into ruins during the Civil War and the flavour that gives it its quaintness to-day is that of the reign of Queen Anne. The prevailing note is struck by the monument to Cornelius Wood, who re-built the church and erected on the north wall in 1707 a large tablet in memory of his parents, Mr. Seth Wood, Minister of the Gospel, and Mistress Elizabeth Wood, his wife. His own monument contains a life-size bust with curling wig in the centre, and all around it a group of military weapons—spears, halberts, swords, pistols—emblematical of the victories of a " late Colonel of a Regiment of Horse and Lieutenant-General of the Armies of Queen Anne." Cupids sport among the piles of cannon-balls, and winged death's heads flit among smiling angels. The same conceits run throughout the building, and angels with gilded wings support the beams of the roof.

Leaving the churchyard we turn to the left. The twisting lane we follow would lead us forward to The Lee; a pleasant village grouped around a well-kept green, where new cottages and new spinneys, mixing so amicably with the old, testify to the late Sir Arthur Liberty's love of beauty in all things. But we take the next turning to the right, and are soon looking into the little valley of The Hale which will bring us down to Wendover. Hills with canopies of beechwoods accompany us on either side, but of Wendover we see nothing till we are close upon it. Where the bottom draws near the main valley a considerable stream gushes out from a spring and we turn to the left to cross it and then take the footpath that follows it down the farther side. We come first to the Manor House and the church, which lie at some little distance from the rest. The church is old but much restored. Many a heretic in the old days was condemned to come and do penance at the Holy Rood of Wendover; the Norman font is interesting and there are good memorials of seventeenth-century Bradshaws. The little stream, bordered on the further side by comfortable-looking houses with gardens, directs us to the centre of the town and we come out at the bottom of the main street.

Leland describes the Wendover of the sixteenth century as " a pretty Through-Fayre Towne, having 2 Streets well builded with Tymbre. . . . The Townlett selfe of Wendover standeth partly upon the North-East Cliffes of Chilterne Hilles. The Residewe and North West Part standeth on the Rootes of the Hilles. Like as the Countrye of the Vale of Alesbury for the most part is cleane barren of Wood, and is champaine; so is all the Chilterne well-wooded and full of Enclosures." His description still holds good. Nowhere is the contrast more marked between the hills with their caps of beechwoods and the open vale, and one descends all the way through it from the " cliffs " to the " roots " before one is fairly in the straight road to Aylesbury. Stevenson, who came here from Peacock Farm, seems to do it less than justice. He calls it " a straggling purposeless sort of place," in which " everyone seems to have had his own opinion as to how the street should go." If he had lived into these days of enlightened town-planning, he would understand the foresight with which the founders removed all fear of future ribbon-development along a straight road, of which glaring examples can be found to-day at no great distance. They laid their main street athwart the track of the Aylesbury road, so that traffic turns right at one end and left at the other, and then filled up the corners;

and they fronted the street with comely houses so well and truly built of mellow bricks and timber that many of them remain to gladden our eyes to-day.

When I first came walking to Wendover, the Red Lion Inn, for which R. L. S. reserves his praises, must have been much as he left it. I remember complimenting the landlord on the charm of the village. " Yes," he said, " but most days you could fire a cannon down the street without hitting anybody." That could seldom happen to-day, and in the general speeding up the inside of the " Red Lion " has been wholly altered. It is probably much more comfortable, but is also more like other inns. The establishment of a great Air Force centre hard by, coupled with the general increase in traffic, has robbed Wendover of its old repose. The French château, which the late Mr. Alfred de Rothschild set up in the very English environment of Halton Park, now flutters with air-marshals, and the symmetrical straight lines of huts, barracks and hangars on the prominent slope do not add to the beauty of the landscape. One hoped that a new Service would have set a new and more æsthetic fashion in planning camps, as they have in their blue-grey uniforms; but here they have been content to follow the lead of the Army school of designers, who, having been set to spend their nights in square barracks and their days on barrack squares while their minds were still plastic, can only think in right-angles.

In the days when the whole county of Yorkshire (outside a few boroughs) only sent two members to the national parliament, Wendover sent exactly the same number. Wendover, as well as Marlow and Amersham, had been represented in the parliaments of the first two Edwards, but the right was allowed to fall into abeyance until the House of Commons began to gain power in the reign of James I. The King was opposed to the increase in the number of members: he said that he was already troubled with too many. But the records in the Tower were searched: the claims of the three little boroughs were upheld, and in 1623 John Hampden became one of the two members for Wendover. The elections were curious affairs, marked by incessant bribery and heavy drinking. On the day of the declaration of the poll at Amersham all the womenfolk of the town collected in the inns, and the newly-elected members visited each inn in turn and solemnly kissed every occupant. But at Wendover drunkenness was always the prevailing feature, and many a member was unseated for bribery. Richard Hampden and Sir Roger Hill were unseated in 1702 but were at once re-elected. They won again by the same means in 1707, and in 1709 the Rev. George Ollyffe was brought over from Great Kimble to preach in Wendover church, for the Society for the Reformation of Manners, against " the excesses and abuses of the several boroughs of the nation at Elections." In the middle of the eighteenth century Earl Verney was landlord of the town, and the tenants paid no rents so long as his candidates were duly elected. But over and above this a vast amount of money had to be spent on entertainment.

The election of 1769, when Edmund Burke was one of Lord Verney's candidates, is the only one of which I have found any contemporary description. It occurs in a book called *John Buncle, junior, Gentleman*, a series of letters describing a journey from London to Stowe in that year. Published anonymously, its author was Dr. Thomas Cogan, the co-founder of the Royal Humane Society:[1]

" Heyday! What is the matter? Behold all the marks of an invasion, or a civil war! Windows broken, doors demolished, sign-posts humbled to the dust! Here stands a man with a broken arm, and yonder go two or three more with bruised face and black eyes! Prithee, what have you all been about? "

" 'Lectioneering, Sir," answers an elderly man, to whom I addressed my enquiry.

" 'Lectioneering, what do you mean by that, good man? "

[1] Some interesting facts about Thomas Cogan are given in Hunter's *Old Age in Bath*. The doctor's brother Eliezer kept the noted academy at High Hill, Walthamstow, attended by the young Benjamin Disraeli. He lived to see his pupil famous, but declared, to the last, " I don't like Disraeli : I never could get him to understand the subjunctive."

" Why it's going about to be made a Parliament man on; and he that gets the most votes carries the day."

" But I do not see the connection, my honest friend, between chusing Mr. A. or Mr. B. for your representative, and demolishing your town, or knocking one another on the head."

" Don't you? why then I can tell you, Meister," says the old gentleman, with a smile of contempt aimed at my ignorance.   " These great fokes makes us little fokes drunk, and when we are drunk we fight, and when we fight we do mischief, that's all."

" The greater fools you to make yourselves such beasts." . . .

" L——d sir, if *you* could get your belly full of vittels and drink for nothing, and money given you into the bargain, you woud now, I'll wornt you.   There is the *White-lyon,* and *Grey-hound,* and *Black-a-more's head,* has been open for these three weeks *successfully.*   Ale was given away by pails-full.   You might go in and eat and drink till you burst again, at ony time, and nobody would take no notice like."—

" So then you are fond of the diversion, I find."

" Alack and a day, sir!   I have lived in the town and paid scot and lot thirty-one years and a half, come Michaelmas next: and I've polled for eleven parliament men, and I've got my swill of ale and a broken pate e'ery time, thank God." . . .

" But pray tell me what these parliament men are good for when you have got them," says Charles, " for on my life I know not."

" Good for, Sir?   Bless your Heart! good for! why if it was not for them we should all be over-run with Papishes and Prespiterians, God knows! "

" And what harm would they do you? "

" Lud, sir, how you talk!   Why, they would knock us on the head, if we did not wear wooden shoes, and go to the Pantile House! "

Thus elected, Edmund Burke sat down to write his *Observations on the Present State of the Nation.*   There is no reason to doubt the general accuracy of Dr. Cogan's picture: that other boroughs were equally bad is a poor excuse. Yet if ever a corrupt tree brought forth good fruit, surely it was Wendover. John Hampden the Patriot sat as its member in five parliaments. That very human genius, Sir Richard Steele, of *The Tatler*, was elected in 1721. By the votes of Wendover Edmund Burke entered parliamentary life in 1765, and George Canning in 1796 first made his mark in handling foreign affairs.

CHAPTER XI

FROM BOXMOOR TO THE CHESS

THE country between the Gade and the Chess is noticeably different from most of the Penn Country. It has a distinct accent of central Hertfordshire. The ground never rises much above 500 feet; soft rounded slopes take the place of abrupt ascents; and only as one rises from the Gade valley or from the Chess is anything of a climb encountered. But it has a charm of its own. Main roads are scarce and no railway has invaded it. It is studded with genuine country villages quite unspoilt, and, though its hollows are mere wrinkles on the surface, they are sufficiently deep and frequent to prevent one from seeing what is coming next, so that a walk across it, by twisting lanes or flowering footpaths, becomes a constant series of pleasant surprises. If the upper heights of the Penn Country have the greater magic, this has its full share of petty witchery.

The stream of the Bulbourne, rising near Northchurch, runs into the Gade near Hemel Hempstead. Boxmoor, on the southern bank, is now growing into a considerable town with paper-mills and other industries, but it affords a quick escape into open country. A hundred yards or so from Boxmoor Station, on the main road to Berkhampstead, we turn to the left at the " Swan," and follow Box Lane through what is evidently the old Boxmoor, with good Georgian houses on either side. Where the houses end, the road continues up a hollow, with the trees of Westbrook Hay prominent on the hill to the right and Sheethanger Common with its golf-links covers the slope on the left. Here we take to the grass, and climbing the common reach at once almost the highest elevation we shall attain. A wood lies before us along the top of the ridge, and, running behind it along the edge of the trees, is a footpath which will take us straight through the fields to Bovingdon.

For a village so near the main road and railway, Bovingdon has been very successful in preserving its rural character. There is no particularly noticeable feature in it. It lies high, with its central cross-roads in a gentle hollow, so that both ends of its pleasantly old-fashioned main street descend towards it. As in the case of so many other villages on the tops of these chalk hills, its water supply was long a source of anxiety, and so late as 1879 a well was sunk in the middle of the cross-roads with an ornamental cover above it, as the most useful memorial to the Hon. Granville Ryder, of Westbrook Hay. It has already been superseded as a water-carrier by the pipes of a water company, but remains as a kind of market cross. Though Bovingdon has had a church for centuries, it is only in modern times that it acquired a vicar of its own. So far back as the year 1235 the vicar of Hemel Hempstead was ordered to serve the chapels of Bovingdon and Flaunden by means of "two fit curates," and this arrangement endured for about six hundred years. Services were supposed to be held monthly, but there were occasions in winter when none were held in three months. Owing to this uncertainty, on the appointed Sunday a man was posted on the church tower to watch the Hemel Hempstead road where it first shows above the ridge. If he saw the parson coming, he came down quickly and rang the bell.

The church was rebuilt in 1845, but some of the older tombs in the churchyard are curious. In a corner, at no great distance from one another, are two with no names attached. Of one, bearing the humble motto "De mortuis nil nisi bonum," nothing seems to be known: the other, simply labelled "Vir Honestus," marks the grave of Sir Nathaniel Gould, of Stoke Newington, a Director of the Bank of England, who died in 1728. A codicil to his will ran as follows: " My body shall be interred in the North-East corner of the churchyard of Bovingdon with a plain Gravestone raised above two feet, and if it

10

please God that I may preserve my Integrity to the end of my days I desire there may be inscribed upon the said Gravestone, Vir Honestus, and nothing else . . . I will have no Escutcheon or other ornaments to attend my ffuneral but only a plain Hearse with three Mourning Coaches and no more, and that two of my Pall Bearers may be yeomen of Bovingdon."

Chipperfield lies to the south-east two miles away, and, by whatever route one elects to cross this watershed, Chipperfield Common must not be missed. The road runs straight to Chipperfield, and carries little traffic, so that we have no need to seek about for a footpath. Fine trees line the hedges for most of the way, and there are pleasant old farm-houses and half-timbered cottages at intervals. We enter Chipperfield through a short street, and, when we emerge at the top of the common, we can scarcely wonder that most of the houses border its northern corner in order to enjoy the view. The common falls downward from our feet in a gentle slope. The stretch of smooth green sward in front, probably cleared from the forest by early residents for pasturage, now forms an ideal village cricket ground, and behind it a low-growing thicket gradually merges into thick woodland. Encroaching on the common to the right the church rises among limes and lofty fir trees, and clumps of birches and oaks against a background of beechwoods complete the amphitheatre. The road by which we came continues forward to Bucks Hill, and through the gap which it cleaves among the trees we see the distant summits of Merry Hill and the ridge that runs from Bushey to Stanmore.

Two ways lie before us. We can plunge forward into the woodlands and strike due south for Sarratt, descending to the Chess at Sarratt Mill; or we can take the road that runs westward by the " Two Brewers," and, bordering another stretch of the common, come to Flaunden and cross the river between Latimer and Chenies. We shall do well to make a three-legged walk of it and follow both.

The call of the high woods across the cricket ground is strong. We will go first by Sarratt; and, taking tracks

SARRATT.

and footpaths, can achieve what no motorist has yet accomplished—come to Sarratt by a straight route. It is a populous village set upon a hill, but so surrounded by a maze of twisting lanes with high hedges that it seems to lie in a little kingdom of its own. You could never pass through it when you were going somewhere else. But the walker can arrive there by walking due south from Chipperfield corner. There are many tracks across Chipperfield Common, all beautiful and each a little different. I will take you by the shortest way, and you can find the variations later. We follow the Bucks Hill road to what appears to be the last house of the village; the fine old manor house lies a little further on, hidden among the trees. But from the red-brick cottage decked with an ancient cherry tree we strike half-right across the grass to an opening in the forest. The path leads us straight to a deep-blue pool surrounded by a ring of venerable lime trees, which stretch out their knotted boughs to meet above it. Here we leave the common by a stile and follow a footpath across the corner of a little park and out of its gate. A lane runs straight forward to a triangular patch of gorse and bracken at Commonwood Common; we leave the road and, following a grassy track down the middle, descend to a lane in the bottom of a hollow. Sarratt lies on the hill in front and a side lane running straight forward quickly takes us to its centre. I know no other village that sets itself quite like this. A long narrow green, with a road on either side, runs for about half a mile along the ridge; and on either side runs a single row of houses, a hundred yards or so apart, as if they were lined up to dance Sir Roger de Coverley. One almost expects the old farm and the post office at the top to join hands and come prancing down the middle past the drum-head well. Here we are on the top of the hog-backed ridge and can see neither end; but, following the line of old-fashioned houses to the left, we soon see the great black barn of Greenend Farm standing right across our path. It is from this end that Mr. Bathurst's drawing is taken. The two old ponds now often run dry in summer: the painted signboard of the " Cricketers'

Arms," with its stalwart sportsmen in white flannels and top-hats, is quite in keeping with the place.

But before we reach the first pond we turn off by a footpath to the right, between the smithy and a row of cottages with high-pitched roofs. We know that Sarratt Church lies at Church End, but look for it in vain at either end of the long village street. For Church End is a separate hamlet three-quarters of a mile away from the middle of Sarratt. Here, as elsewhere in Chiltern nomenclature, "End" has the old and obsolete meaning that only survives in common talk in the expression " odds and ends "—an end that has no beginning but is a bit cut off. Martins End, near Great Missenden, is said to have once belonged to Mayertorne Manor, half-way to Wendover, and the many other Chiltern Ends were similarly isolated bits of land lying in the midst of other people's property. To-day, with the redistribution of estates, it means no more than a hamlet.

The footpath we have chosen runs parallel to the lane, but gives infinitely finer views, for, passing through a wood, we come out on the top of a bank descending to the Chess in its most attractive reach. There are few more beautiful scenes than a river turning a corner in a wooded valley, and the bend of the Chess round Mount Wood holds high rank among the views of the Penn Country. From here we can almost see round the corner, and follow the valley beyond the park of Latimer to the hills above Chesham, and all the way one wood after another descends the slope. It was these woods that so delighted William Cobbett, riding over the hill to Amersham: he found a great resemblance to those he had known in Long Island during his exile in the United States: but he thought the American woods more varied. This may be true of the woods themselves, which are mostly beech; but from where we sit we cannot complain of lack of variety in the general view of the valley. The oaks in the bottom have already turned yellow; silver-grey willows line the stream curling down the bottom: the elms rising about a red-brick farm have as yet only attained their first pale green phase; and behind them all a russet background of beeches.

With many a glance backward at the Crook of Chess, we follow our path through a field of pale-blue roots which ends at the churchyard gate under a spreading yew tree.

Sarratt Church is interesting both in its shape and in its materials. It has a saddleback roof and large transepts, and its tower has a gabled top, giving together an outline of many angles. Mainly built of flints in the traditional Chiltern manner, there are great puddingstones inserted here and there at the foot of the walls, and in the tower the flints give way to ancient brickwork near the top. Some of the bricks are of that narrow shape that always suggests the handiwork of Roman builders. The inside appears as angular as the roof; the chief features are the finely carved Jacobean pulpit and the memorial in which William Kyngsley, Knt. (1502) kneels at a prayer-desk with his wife, with their four sons and one daughter behind them. The age of the church is unknown, but it first appears in history eleven centuries and more ago, when Offa, King of the Mercians, gave it to the Abbey of St. Albans. I have spoken of Sarratt as a sequestered, out-of-the-world sort of place; for Sarratt Church End one can only double the adjectives. Apart from the mansion of Goldingtons, there is only a little row of almshouses, founded in 1550 and rebuilt in 1821, an inn, and a great double-gabled barn of black timbers abutting on the churchyard. Small wonder that such seclusion led to independent thinking. A fifteenth-century vicar, with leanings towards Lollardy, was ejected for " apostasy," and in later days there were many Quakers in the district. The eminent Nonconformist divine, Richard Baxter, who had previously escaped from the London plague to be the guest of Richard Hampden at Hampden House and thus knew something of the Chilterns, became much exercised about this second outbreak of heresy. " The country about Rickmersworth," he writes, " abounding with Quakers because Mr. W. Pen, their captain, dwelleth there, I was desirous that the poor people should once hear what was to be said for their recovery ": and for ten consecutive Sundays he preached in local churches against it. One of these churches was Sarratt.

Opposite the churchyard a footpath, crossing the drive of Goldingtons, runs down the steep hill to the old corn-mill of Sarratt, and there turns to the left to join the lane near the bridge. Mount Wood and the river bend are still part of the attractive picture we enjoy as we descend, but a new view opens out down the valley to the left, ended by Oxhey Woods beyond Rickmansworth. If we cross the bridge and follow the lane up the hill we can soon reach Chorleywood Station: but a riverside walk is a rarity in the Penn Country, and, beyond the first cottage across the Chess, we can find a footpath running to the left which will take us on the grass all the way to Rickmansworth. This path encounters many lanes, and seldom goes straight across them: in any case of doubt one can find the way forward by following the lane towards the river. In the three miles from Sarratt Mill to Rickmansworth, there is only one short portion—where the main road comes near the river and much building is in progress on the Loudwater estate—that has in any way lost its charm. At the start we have two miles of perfect country, with great beechwoods falling down the slopes to the willows and bulrushes below, and we end through a fine open stretch of Rickmansworth Park.

We must now hark back to Chipperfield and try the alternative route. The road to Flaunden runs surprisingly straight past Chipperfield Church and along the edge of the common, but before long it begins to conform to local custom, and there are many twists and turns to be negotiated before we take a sharp corner into the main street. Flaunden lies high on a spur, two miles north of Sarratt Church End, with its not too attractive church on the end, looking down upon the valley. It was built in 1838 and probably occupies its prominent position owing to the great difficulty the curates from Hemel Hempstead always had in finding the old one, of which the remains lie, half-hidden by a wood, not far from the bank of the Chess in the valley below. It would seem that for a time Flaunden was churchless: for the county historian, Clutterbuck, writing in 1815 describes the old church as " a mean structure . . . partly inhabited by poor families." It is now a complete ruin, open to the sky and much damaged by ivy; its fine font alone was preserved and placed in the new church. Straight from the church we descend into a deep bottom, a natural feature so rare in this country of indefinite slopes and little hollows that it has been chosen as the county boundary. In place of the constant twists of high-hedged lanes, we can step out boldly on the open road down the curving vale, with the left foot in Hertfordshire and the right in Buckingham-shire to make a county match of it. Shortly before we reach the main Chess valley, we pass through the little black-and-white hamlet of Latimer, and soon see Latimer House rising among the trees on the hill to our right.

The place was called Isenhampstead till a family named Latimer became lords of the manor in the fourteenth century. It then became Isenhampstead Latimer, and finally Latimer. After the departure of the Latimers, several families in succession became the owners. From the Grevilles it passed to the Sandys family, during whose tenure it was the birthplace of a remarkable old lady in-cluded by Thomas Fuller among the Worthies of Bucking-hamshire. This was Hester, daughter of Myles Sandys, who became wife of Sir Thomas Temple and mother of the first builder of Stowe. " She had," says Fuller, " four sons and nine daughters which lived to be married, and so exceedingly multiplied that this lady saw seven hundred extracted from her body. Reader, I speak within compass, and have left myself a reserve, having bought the truth hereof by a wager I lost." Lady Temple was eighty-seven when she died in 1656. During her lifetime Latimer passed to the great family of Cavendish, then earls of Devonshire: here Christiana, Countess of Devonshire, en-tertained Charles I when a prisoner of the Parliamentary army; and the same house was one of Charles II's places of refuge when he was escaping from the country after Worcester. Horace Walpole visited Latimer in 1749 and 1755 and notes considerable alterations made to it in the interval. On the first occasion he was visiting his cousins, the Conways, who had rented it. " This house," he writes, " is large and bad, old but of a bad age: finely situated on a hill in a beechwood with a river at the bottom, and a range of hills and woods on the opposite side belonging to the Bedfords. They are fond of it; the view is melancholy." He paid his second visit from Chalfont Park, when the owners had returned, and found it " much improved." It is difficult to-day to understand how anyone could call this prospect " melancholy "; but the kind of country which the eighteenth century condemned as " unimproved," we praise to-day as " unspoilt." The present owner of Latimer House is Lord Chesham, head of a younger branch of the Cavendish family.

Crossing the bridge over the Chess we strike at right-angles a road that follows the valley. If we turned to the right, it would lead us to Chesham four miles away: in the first mile it crosses part of the site of a Roman villa, of which a considerable portion, with a fine tessellated pavement, has been found in the adjoining garden. But we take the road to the left and climb the hill to the little village of Chenies, owned for four centuries by the house of Russell, earls and dukes of Bedford. The pleasant red-gabled houses are for the most part grouped round a village green, shaded by lofty trees, with a well in the centre. Close at hand stands the inn, visited by the historian Froude in 1879, when he came to catch fish and muse on that Great Subject—the progress of the house of Russell. He delighted in the peaceful village, but his Tory spirit could not resist a gibe at its Whig owners:

" All is old-fashioned, grave and respectable. No signs are to be found of competition, of the march of intellect, of emancipation, of the divine right of each man and woman to do what is good in their own eyes—of the blessed liberty which the House of Russell has been so busy in setting forward. The inhabitants of Cheneys live under authority. The voice of the Russells has been the voice of the emancipator, the hand that of a ruling noble. . . ."

A short road running from the green leads to the church on the right, and straight forward to a much re-

stored and rebuilt manor house. Chenies passed from the
Cheyney family, to whom it owes its name, to the Sap-
cotes, and came to the Russells in 1526 by the marriage of
John Russell, first Earl of Bedford, to the Sapcote heiress.
Thenceforward we can trace the vicissitudes of the man-
sion in the accounts of many a traveller. The first pic-
ture of it under Russell rule comes from Leland in 1538:
" The old House of Cheyneis is so translated by Lord
Russell, that hath this house in right of his wife, that
little or nothing remaineth untranslated; and a great deal
of the house is even newly set up, made of brick and
timber." The second Earl was much perturbed when
Queen Elizabeth decided to pay him a visit: " I understand
Her Majesty's coming to Chenies " (he writes to Lord
Burleigh) : " where if the house was sweet and the lodging
commodious I should be glad thereof: but as to the soil
and seat thereof, as no art nor diligence can amend nature's
doings, so I am sorry that it cannot now be amended, if
even it might be for a time, to ease thereby so noble a
guest and so large a train." Francis, the fourth Earl, was
called " the Wise "; he employed the Dutchman Vermuy-
den to begin the draining of the Fens by digging the Bedford levels, receiving from the King a grant of many a
thousand acres, and he died in 1641, in time to avoid the
ruin brought by the Civil War upon so many great and
wealthy families. Thenceforward the fortunes of the
Russells were closely intertwined with those of the Cavendish family of Latimer; both houses rebelled against the
French-Catholic intrigues of the restored Stuarts, and both
together were granted dukedoms by William and Mary.
With the building of the new Woburn Abbey in the following century the Manor House at Chenies fell on evil
days. Horace Walpole deplored its condition in 1749.
" There are but piteous fragments of the house remaining,
now a farm, built round three sides of a court. It is
dropping down, in several places without a roof, but in
half the windows are beautiful arms in painted glass. As
these are so totally neglected, I propose making a push
and begging them of the Duke of Bedford. They would
be magnificent for Strawberry Castle . . ." The house

never regained its former importance. A part of it has been restored and largely rebuilt, and for many years it has been the residence of the principal farmer on this portion of the Bedford estate.

St. Michael's Church, which lies under the wing of the Manor House, is from the outside an attractive building. Within it appears lopsided, for the part seems greater than the whole. The eye cannot fail to be distracted from the main building to the Russell Chapel, which occupies the entire north aisle. Arches filled with glass windows separate it from the nave, and through them the ermine and red velvet of earl and countess, duke and duchess, put the rest of the church into the shade. We cannot enter the chapel: the key would have to be brought all the way from Woburn by some high official: we can only gaze through the windows. Since Walpole's time, " the house of Russell robed in alabaster and painted " has had many additions, and the chapel seems nearly full. At the east end, side by side on their tomb, lie John, first Earl of Bedford and his Countess, who built this chapel in 1556 in accordance with his will, and a long line follows them down the aisle. Two slabs of black marble mark the tomb of Lord John Russell, the champion of the great Reform Bill and afterwards Prime Minister. The west wall is nearly covered by an immense monument to the first Duke and Duchess of Bedford, with medallion portraits of their children. This is the tomb condemned by Froude as an atrocious outrage on good taste: it is unpleasantly melodramatic. In the middle is the portrait of their eldest son, Lord William Russell, condemned by an illegally constituted court and on perjured evidence, and executed to become the martyr of the Glorious Revolution; and from it his parents turn away in attitudes of uncontrollable grief. We cannot read the names on many of the monuments, but we know that all are Russells or their near relations. In the nave outside are a few brasses earlier than the chapel, one of a member of the Cheyney family. In this church's history there is only one figure that could hold its own against all the Bedfords: here in 1630 the great Lady Anne Clifford, Countess of Dorset,

who ruled her northern castles so imperiously, took Philip
Earl of Pembroke for her second husband.

The main road from Rickmansworth to Amersham lies
a few hundred yards to the south; we can enter it about
half-way between the stations of Chorleywood and Chalfont Road. But its recent " improvement " into a hedgeless main road with pavements like a seaside esplanade has
made it uninviting to pedestrians. A better walking route
to Chorleywood will be found by descending a lane on the
further side, and in the bottom of the valley beyond take
the footpath that runs to the left through woods and
fields. For Chalfont Road we had better retrace our
steps up the Chess Valley, and in place of crossing the
river to Latimer keep forward to Dell Farm. Here is a
footpath on the left running up the hill and through the
wood on the top; we can thence come straight to the
station without touching a road all the way.

CHAPTER XII

BETWEEN THE OXFORD ROADS

WEST of the Risborough gap the main ridge of the Chilterns runs unbroken to the river. No railway has pierced or climbed it, and the two roads that take the Londoner to Oxford without a wide détour have to climb laboriously to the summit and descend precipitous slopes to the vale beyond. Between these two lies a country little known: a jumble of narrow valleys and thickly wooded hills, where the lanes come to their destination by starting in the opposite direction and only footpaths take you fairly straight to anywhere. Little Norman churches rise from little hidden villages, and its wealth of wild flowers has not yet been devoured, roots and all, by the swarm of locusts that comes in chars-à-bancs. I place its pole or centre at the old windmill that looks down upon Turville on one side and Fingest on the other. It is still a little sanctuary of unspoilt country, and, if I reveal to you some small fragments of its secrets, I conjure you, in the names of all the ancient gods, not to spoil it.

The few people I have met who know and love this patch of England undefiled mostly found it by losing themselves: they were trying to get to somewhere quite ordinary and fell into it by mistake. As a thoroughfare to anywhere it is frankly impossible. Many years ago a foreigner who knew no better traversed it as the nearest way from London to Oxford. This was Brunetto Latini from Florence, Dante's tutor; but, when he won through to the vale beyond and rested at the moated castle of Shirburn, he told such tales of " hills of hazardous ascent, bad roads, dense woods full of robbers who for blackmail were connived at by the Barons," that their horror has deterred

156

all imitators for these six centuries. Nor is one likely to find it by straying from either of the Oxford highways. The traveller by Henley and Benson is not far off at Nettlebed, but the lanes that follow the narrow intervening valleys all run crossways—they mostly come from Devil's Hill at Russell's Water—and by cunning, imperceptible curves lure him back to Henley. The nearest entry from the Wycombe-Stokenchurch road is subtly camouflaged behind the factory chimney that rises so out of place in the quiet hamlet of Piddington. A motorbus from High Wycombe has lately come to take this route, passing through Fingest and Hambleden, but few passengers seem to go beyond Lane End or to descend at the right places. Its infrequent passage does little to disturb the ancient peace of the Hambleden valley, and it takes the walker quickly to his starting-points. Quite a number of Wycombe buses come by various routes as far as Lane End, a populous village that sits astride the watershed between the Wycombe and the Hambleden valley systems, and, having shops, is the little metropolis of the district. This is probably the most convenient approach to the upper valley, but the natural entry is to start from the Thames and ascend by the little stream that rises below Turville and joins the river near Hambleden Mill.

Here we start on solid ground. The old weather-boarded mill is well known to all who take their pleasure on the river. Hambleden lock, close by, ends the reach that contains the course of Henley regatta; and the road that follows the river from Marlow to Henley makes this little group of buildings familiar to the motorist. But few notice the lesser road that here strikes northwards. Right at the outset we find something interesting and something odd. The old manor house of Yewden, with its six gables and garden walls of clipped yew trees, faces the road just round the corner. It has centuries of history behind it; but there are fields at the back with traces of antiquity far more remote. Here have been discovered very complete remains of the farm of a provincial Roman. The whole area was carefully excavated and closely studied by experts who assigned to every building its proper functions. The remains have now been covered up again, but a wonderful model is shown in the little archæological museum up the road. There we see the mansion of the owner, the houses of his servants, and the walls of his paddocks. Especially interesting are the great granaries: the ingenious Roman, finding the climate here less kind than in his native Italy, had fitted a number of furnaces beneath the floors to dry and ripen the corn and so complete the work that nature had left undone. Round the walls of the museum are ranged tiles, fragments of mosaic, and strange implements of daily use, with a specimen furnace in the midst; and one marvels at the skill and knowledge which have enabled archæologists to reconstruct the life on a Roman farm from such materials. But one discovery has baffled them. It would need an expert in blacker magic than theirs to explain how numbers of babies' skeletons came to be buried in a corner of the croft.

Hambleden village lies a mile from the river, standing back under the hill on a by-pass away from the main road, which gives it all the peacefulness of a Thames backwater. The Manor, which stands at the east end of the village with its back to the hill, is a many-gabled Jacobean house of dressed flint, an unusual combination. It was built in 1604 by Emanuel Scrope, afterwards Lord Scrope of Bolton, and sheltered the fugitive Charles I in 1646. The church opposite its gate has been much restored, but, though antiquaries of the severer kind may condemn it as patchwork, apart from the unpleasing tower the contributions of different ages are by no means inharmonious, and, with elms and cedars about it, it takes its place not unworthily among the old houses of the village. As we enter the narrow nave near the west end, the church seems small for the wide extent of its ancient parish; but, as we advance towards the chancel, spacious transepts open on either side, and it looks too large for its scattered population. Apart from the Norman font, which is said to have held the water for Simon de Montfort's christening, the most interesting portion is the north transept. Here are ancient brasses of the Shipwash family, surmounted by their shield displaying a demi-lamb struggling out of

Charles f Bathurst 1928

HAMBLEDEN.

curling waves of heraldic sheep-dip and beside them is the
altar tomb erected in 1633 to Sir Cope D'Oyley and his
wife.   Alabaster effigies are not uncommon in this district:
we shall meet with more magnificent examples at Rotherfield Greys and Ewelme; but this group of the D'Oyley
family seems to me more actual, more lifelike, than any.
The parents kneel face to face in the centre with their
children on either side—the sons behind the father and the
daughters behind the mother, two by two; and every face
is so full of character, all with a family likeness but still
so different, that one cannot doubt that they are good
portraits by a very competent artist.   Some of the
children had died before their parents, and carry skulls in
their hands.   In these very clothes we can picture them
all demurely issuing from the manor gate, and kneeling
just so in the manor pew.   Francis Quarles, the Royalist
poet, was Lady D'Oyley's brother, and wrote the epitaphs
on the base of the tomb: that to his sister Martha is typical
of the quaint conceits of the author of the *Emblems,* and
runs as follows:

> " Wouldst thou, reader, draw to life,
> The perfect copy of a wife,
> Read on ; and then redeem from shame
> That lost but honourable name.
> This was once in spirit a Jael,
> Rebecca in grace, in heart an Abigail ;
> In works a Dorcas, to the church a Hanna,
> And to her spouse Susanna.
> Prudently simple, providently wary,
> To the world a Martha, to heaven a Mary."

To the south of the church is the little *place* of the
village, shaded by spreading trees, as you see it in Mr.
Bathurst's drawing.   The old houses stand at ease in
irregular groups about it, and the only semblance of a
street runs from the corner for some thirty yards and
leads no further than the Rectory gate.   The sign of the
" Stag and Huntsman " is conspicuous on its right-hand
side—a name that recalls the days when the Royal Buck-
hounds used to hunt this district: old inhabitants still talk
of a famous run from Stonor Park in 1861.   Many visitors

return to stay here every summer, and find new walks each year.

The next village up the valley is Skirmett, two miles away from Hambleden, a tiny place that lies along both sides of the road. The Old Crown Inn, a picturesque house with many little gables, sits back from the street, and most of the cottage gardens are gay with flowers. Already a narrow hill crowned by a white windmill has appeared in the centre of the valley before us, the tip of a long spur that runs back, with little increase in width, to the Chiltern summit near Stokenchurch. When we reach the foot of the hill the road divides, the valley splits into four. Eastward a bottom runs up to Bolter End and Lane End, westward to Turville Heath; and two deep dales, thickly wooded at the further end, run forward on either side the central spur. Close on our right lies Fingest; round the corner on the left is Turville.

I first came to Turville and Fingest on the wheels of chance. It was in the time when so many people used to drive bicycles with their own legs—an age that now seems almost as remote as the days when donkeys, by the same motive power, drew water from our Chiltern wells. The three of us had pushed the things up Dashwood Hill, and pedalling through Stokenchurch turned to the left where the Oxford Road descends by Aston Rowant Wood. Thenceforward we pursued the glorious by-road that runs along the escarpment with uninterrupted views of the multi-coloured plain where the vales of Thame and Thames and White Horse merge into one. The day was hot and sunny; we sat on Bald Hill to eat our lunch and enjoy the prospect, and then pushed on to Christmas Common. There somebody said, " Here's a lane on the left pointing our way; let's try it! " As it seemed to lead downhill we all assented. We were aiming for High Wycombe as the first point on our homeward road, but the wheels took charge. We went gently past North End —a pleasant corner with plenty of open grass and a pond reflecting an old farm-house behind it—and where the principal road turned off to the right we let the wheels run on. The descent grew steeper and the pace increased:

we found ourselves carried down a little sunken lane. The banks on either side rose high above us and the trees met densely overhead, for all the world like one of those river tunnels by which romancers take their heroes into strange and unknown countries. As the trench (it was little more) grew narrower, faster and faster we flew—thank Heaven we didn't meet a haycart!—and when we reached the bottom and could look about us the impetus carried us on through alternating patches of hot sunshine and sombre woodlands down the bottom of a quiet little valley. When the wheels stopped we found ourselves in Turville.

We were already anxious about getting home, but there was something about the place that held us. The row of gabled cottages was smothered by wistaria in full bloom; the old church beneath its trees was just suited to the place, and, on the long green down above, a white windmill shone like a lighthouse on a dangerous cape. But the charm was not in this or that detail, but in the whole. The village was strangely silent: we had not met a soul since Christmas Common and nobody stood about the cottage doors. The spell was still upon us when we rounded Windmill Cape and came without warning upon Fingest Church, a building so remarkable that one wonders how it escaped becoming famous. Equally reticent was the little village that breathed antiquity along two sides of the churchyard. The hill to Bolter End was steep and long, but, thinking of what we had seen, we all felt that the ascent was worth the effort. It is difficult to recall with truthfulness one's first impressions of a place with which one has since become familiar. As we pushed our bicycles up the road, one mentioned one feature, another was more impressed by another; but we all agreed upon its peculiar " difference " from anywhere else, and I think we all felt that we must come again. And again.

To revisit such a place often brings disillusionment, but every time I return to the Fingest country its enchantment grips me more firmly. Nor have I ever taken a walk around it without discovering some new beauty. Once you begin to know the little lanes and footpaths you can drop into this hollow from any point of the compass. You can strike north over Cadmore End Common, where it crosses the Piddington road, and fetching a compass by Cadmore End descend through Hanger Wood; you can come from Stonor and South End on the west, or follow the narrow ridge by Ibstone all the way from Stokenchurch till, reaching its final tip by Turville windmill, you look down upon Turville village just as you see it in Mr. Bathurst's drawing. There is much of interest in Turville Church, stone figures of men in armour, carved woodwork of very venerable age, ancient coffins. Fingest Church, too, always draws me, with its great square Norman tower wider than nave and chancel. The interior has been spoilt by excessive restoration, but the tower looks equally imposing whether seen at a distance as one enters the valley from Bolter End, or rising above old roofs from the garden of the Chequers Inn across the road, which happens to lie in the next parish. It was when I was seeking another point of view that I chanced to light upon a little croft behind it, surrounded by venerable walls with curious brickwork. That is all that remains of the ancient palace of the Bishops of Lincoln. For centuries their diocese stretched from the Humber to the Thames, and this was the ultimate point of an episcopal progress.

The best approach to Fingest is not on the level from Hambleden or Turville, but by a footpath over the hill from Frieth. From Lane End it is an easy descent to Moorend Common, and Frieth lies on the hill straight ahead. Follow the village street past the church, and, right at the end, before the road divides to Parmoor and to Skirmett, take a lane to the right, on the near side of the last farmyard in Frieth. This lane runs straight across a field, and when it bends to the right, go forward by a rough cart-road between hedges. In a field at the far end where a footpath leads straight into Mousells Wood, choose the track that skirts the wood to the left and enter it at the far corner. Crossing a clearing in its centre, we descend a little way through larches and then emerge into the open. The meeting-place of many valleys lies beneath us, with the white windmill standing out upon its hill

FINGEST AND THE TURVILLE VALLEY FROM MOUSELLS HILL.

in the centre and Fingest at its foot. This particular prospect seems to me and to others to epitomize, so far as such a thing is possible, the enchantment that clings to us wherever we walk among these valleys. It is not merely the beauty of the view—the graceful folding of the hills, the shape and silence of the woods. Nor is it only the decorous antiquity of the villages, though their ancient glories have been revealed by experts in place-name study. To me, who have sat here in early spring and seen the tall church tower rising above the leafless elms, Fingest must always mean that superlative finger pointing upwards. More learned men say that it was once called Thinghurst, the seat of a Thing, or parliament, and Skirmett was Shire-meet, the gathering-place of some unrecorded county council; and that must be quite a long time ago. But the spell is cast by something above and beyond all this—a charm, a magic older than the stone coffins in Turville Church, older than Christianity itself. Mr. Rudyard Kipling has told us how the People of the Hills, the Old Things, flitted from Sussex before the relentless march of new ideas: I am sure they linger still in woods round Turville.

St. Birinus the Lombard is always called the apostle of the Chilterns. He christened converts in Bapsey Meadow by Taplow, and from Howe Hill or Swyncombe Downs, not far from here, we can gaze over the lowland fields of Dorchester, the seat of his episcopal see. But the only spot near these remoter valleys with which history connects his name is Berin's Hill beyond Stoke Row. Now Berin's Hill is but half-way up the Chiltern slope, barely on the fringe of the woodlands, and almost within hail of the cities of the plain. Can it be that he got no further in his preaching and returned, like an airman, to report that he had dropped his bombs with marked effect? Tradition asserts that he died from the bite of a viper encountered in the Chiltern woods, so he may have tried again; but place-names help the belief that he never penetrated far. Close against his hill lies the wood still called the Devil's Churchyard, and, just over the ridge towards Stonor, Devil's Hill rises from Russell's Water

Common. In the north country they apply this diabolic title quite loosely to anything particularly strange, uncouth or monstrous: there " Devil's Bridge " is no more than a politer form for " the devil of a bridge." But there is nothing peculiar about this Devil's Hill: the name falls pat into its place in the mass of Chiltern nomenclature derived from early owners—Chipps's Farm and Balham's Wood; Plomer's Green and Sprig's Alley; Wheeler End and Mallard's Court; Devil's Hill and Bryant's Bottom. You catch the lilt of it? Just so they sang the roll-call when the Chancellor mounted the woolsack in Fingest. This devil, of course, is not the unlovable fiend who prowls about the streets of towns, but a devil turned country gentleman, who assumed the additional name of Pan on succeeding to the property; a staunch Conservative, preserving wild creatures in his woods, severe on trespassers. Once upon a time the people of Ibstone, which lies on the ridge behind that windmill, conceived the idea of building a new church for their village in a three-cornered field below, up the Turville valley. A neat edifice, one feels sure: pebble-dashed brown plaster, pink asbestos roof and transparencies in the windows. But the walls they built up by day were all thrown down by night. They had to give in at last, and old Ibstone Church still hides among the trees on the top of Ibstone Common. On the three-cornered field in the valley below the Ordnance Map writes, with all the weight of official authority—" Hellcorner Farm."

Then there is a curious tale about a Bishop of Lincoln. It was recorded, *circa* 1340, by Brother Thomas Walsingham of the Abbey of St. Albans: he used to sit in the refectory, listening to the stories of passing travellers, and wrote them down on parchment. His monkish Latin may be roughly translated as follows:

" About that time Henry Burghersh, bishop of Lincoln, ended his last day at Ghent in Flanders: he was succeeded by Thomas le Bek, a noble and excellent clerk. This Henry, former bishop of Lincoln, being greedy and avaricious, had made a park at his farm at ' Tynghurst,' and had added to the same park the neighbouring lands of his tenants, against their will, and had enclosed them with hedges and ditches: not without their dire curses had he entered into his new property.   But after his death he appeared to one of his former squires with bow and quiver, arrows and horn, and clad in a short tunic and that green, and said to him: ' Know that not without offence to God and injustice to the poor did I enclose that park: I am therefore, as a punishment, put in charge of that park, as you see, until the enclosed land be restored to its own possessors.   Go, therefore, to thy brethren, the canons of Lincoln, and beg them on my behalf that all these things be restored to their old possessors, from whom I unjustly took them.'   The canons, hearing this and not being ignorant of the injustice, sent one of their canons, William called ' Bacheler,' to restore to each his own, to dig up the hedges and flatten the ditches.   Who, returning by way of the Abbey of St. Albans, related all these things in order . . ."

Bow and arrows, horn and quiver, green jerkin!   Where did the bishop borrow these properties?   Surely the finger of Pan was in this business too.[1]

Pondering these things I came one midday to Turville in search of local information and found an old gentleman at his cottage door.   He had only come there forty-eight years ago, and inclined to the untenable heresy that Hell-corner meant no more than Hill-corner.   But he made full amends by telling me the odd story of the Sleeping Girl of Turville.   When he first came there, in

[1] If you want more recent knowledge of this likeable demon I can only refer you to an excellent book I have lately read called *Lolly Willowes* by Miss Sylvia Townsend Warner.   It is partly about a remote Chiltern village called Old Mop.   Her plot is a matter-of-fact story about a lady who went to live there and became a witch—the kind of thing that might happen in these parts at any change of the moon.   But her description of the secrets of the woods, of the runes chanted by the night-wind on the hilltop, and of all the moods that follow on from cowslip-time to gold and russet autumn, puts into living words that intangible something that most of us can only feel in such a country.

one of the ancient houses by the churchyard a girl had been sleeping seven years. She had gone to sleep as a schoolgirl and was then a grown woman. People came from all parts to see her, and the old half-timbered Bull and Butcher Inn down the street flourished exceedingly. She eventually woke up when three months short of the tenth anniversary. There was a change of houses about Christmas time; she opened her eyes in the cold air as they carried her across the street, and was soon walking about as if nothing had happened. A curious incident occurred during her slumber. Her mother fell downstairs and died from the shock; and my informant was summoned to serve on the jury at the inquest. I was shown the window in the brick-and-timber gable lighting the little room upstairs where they all assembled. The coroner was there, the doctor, the policeman, the twelve jurymen and several witnesses; and all the time the Sleeping Girl lay sleeping on a bed in the corner.

The old gentleman paused, searching his memory for further details, and I looked up and down the quiet street. On the patch of green beside the churchyard hedge a white dog lay extended on its side. Not a leaf stirred in the Rectory garden, and the sails of the windmill, peeping above the cottage roof, were motionless. By the little sawmill, where the road vanishes in the wood like an unlit passage, a workman, his luncheon done, was leaning back, cap over eyes, against the wall. There seemed no other sign of life. Then the story ended: " And it's because of that girl that neighbours sometimes call us Sleepy Turville."

In the days when Fingest and Turville were centres of government and commerce, I always think that their West End—not only in sober geographical fact but in social importance—must have been up on the hill at Turville Heath. It is not only the air of the place; you can guess it from the map. For if you see a hamlet called North End on one side and another called South End on the other, something important must always have lain between. And there, in the middle, sits Turville Heath.

Charles J. Bathurst 1928

TURVILLE.

You can reach it from Turville by many ways. You can follow the road through Turville to North End, and turn to the left at the pond; or you can take a road that runs off to the right just south of the village and curving up a rising bottom arrives by Summer Heath; or you can take a footpath that leaves the little green between two cottages near the church, and follow the spur upwards by Turville Court. You will know that you have got there when the road passes between two lines of ancient trees that form an avenue of uncommon beauty a quarter of a mile in length. If you have arrived from North End, the heath, or common, lies on the left, and little pathways break away continually through the gorse and foxgloves, where residents have blazed their trails to their own homes, scattered along the further side. On the right, unfenced from road or common, lies the mansion of Turville Park, with its actual park covering a spur to the south and giving views of incredible distance across the Berkshire hills. The present house was built in the eighteenth century by William Perry, who married a co-heiress of the Earls of Leicester; and it has been much altered since. But the original building at Turville Park must have been a very old one, for its well was sunk in the days of Edward II. When it was cleaned out in recent years the date 1308 was found on the wall near the bottom of the shaft, idly scratched by one of the workmen who made it. A well such as this, driven 350 feet deep in solid chalk, could only have been made by a master of plentiful labour, and even in Arthur Young's day it remained the sole dependable supply for a large district. It is an article of local faith that the ghost of a certain Lady Brandon still haunts the park, and the Brandons exercised authority hereabouts in the sixteenth century. She is noteworthy for the perfection of her ghostly manners. She never wails or tears her hair or pops out on you in the dark: you only know that she is there by the rustling of her silken gown.

The present house has had its interesting residents. Here came in 1840 Disraeli's friend, Lord Chancellor Lyndhurst, to add another name to the long list of statesmen who have sought rest and recreation in the Penn Country. He leased it for fourteen years, enjoying his garden, his books and a little gentle agriculture. He kept 100 sheep, four cows, and some 80 head of poultry, " so that you will perceive " (writes his sister) " we are very great farmers." An earlier tenant was that curious Frenchman, General Dumouriez, who after serving in the armies of Kings Louis XV and XVI, was induced by ambition to join the Jacobins at the outbreak of the Revolution. Having led the Revolutionary army to victory over the Austrians at Jemappes, he changed again; and after a futile attempt to overthrow the Convention he escaped abroad and intrigued in turn on behalf of the Bourbons and of their Orleanist rivals. Eventually drifting to England, in return for a pension he assisted the British War Office in planning campaigns against his native country. He enjoyed a considerable social success in Ealing; but one cannot think he would be so welcome to the faithful People of the Hills. Perhaps they put him on a year's probation. He arrived at Turville Park at 2.30 p.m. on March 14, 1822; he died there at 2.30 p.m. on March 14, 1823. There is a tablet to his memory in Henley Church.

The road that traverses the avenue goes straight forward across an open common to Summer Heath, and will take you either to South End or down the hill to Fingest. But we will make a short detour into Oxfordshire to visit Stonor. In the dip where the great trees end and the new little church occupies a corner of the park we turn to the right, and descend a steep valley, till the road runs up against a giant wall of beeches, the outer hoof of the great horseshoe of wooded hills that surrounds Stonor Park. Rounding this obstacle by complicated curves we pass the park gate to see the beauties of the village. It lies in a quiet valley with a steep fir-clad hill rising from its back doors, every cottage built in local style of local material. The gardens are bright with flowers, roses climb the walls, and an air of peace and restfulness lies upon it. The little row of almshouses, built of brick and flint, with dormer windows winking from the tiled roof,

are said to have had their origin in a wager between
Stonor and a Vansittart: the loser to build them and endow
them with £50 a year in perpetuity. But Stonor is a
place to see, not to talk about, and we return to take the
footpath that enters Stonor Park on the near side of the
main gate. This enviable demesne belongs to Lord Camoys,
head of the Stonor family and descendant of John de
Stonor, to whom Edward I granted a charter of Free
Warren in 1295. Leland, in the days of Henry VIII,
called it " a fayre park and a warren of conies and a
fayre wood." It lies, as has been said, in a horseshoe of
wooded hills, with the gates in the centre of the opening,
the drive running up the bottom, and all the rest falling
down towards them. Our footpath runs along the slope
on the right and gives an excellent view of the house,
which sits low on the opposite hill. The old mansion,
where Father Campion and many a Roman Catholic
fugitive sheltered in the days of persecution, has been replaced by a long low house of red brick, with the old
walled gardens above it—a building fully endowed with
that elusive quality architects call " repose." Following the
curve of the horseshoe we re-enter the drive and ascend
the hill through the woods to the back gate, where we step
back out of Oxfordshire into Bucks and find ourselves
on South End Common. It is a scene of quiet beauty,
a picture that composes itself. Some half a dozen old
farm-houses and cottages stand at intervals around a
stretch of turf, with here and there a patch of gorse and
bracken. Except for the great oak in the corner by the
Drover Inn, the only trees upon it are a striking group of
three tall ashes in the centre, leaning together to whisper
ancient secrets across a pool.

At the far side of the common is a lane which soon
becomes a footpath; Turville Hill with its windmill stands
out below us and we can quickly descend to Fingest.
Or we can turn to the right at the park gate and follow the
winding lane through to Fawley. Wild flowers are with
us all the way, the startling blue of chicory beneath the
hedge, spikes of tawny mullein rising among brambles,
and finally, as we come through a grove of oak trees

down to the Thames, in every clearing a blaze of pinky-purple loosestrife, known in these parts as " Children of the Wood." We emerge on the main road not far from Henley. Whichever way we have chosen, we shall have a happy ending to a good day.

CHAPTER XIII

OVER THE OXFORDSHIRE BORDER

AS one follows the Thames upwards from Taplow, the wooded spur of the Chilterns which rises straight from its eastern bank comes to an abrupt end where the Wycombe Valley joins the river and the heights of Hedsor slope steeply down to Cookham weir. For a time the hills withdraw on our right, till, close behind Marlow, a great chalk bluff of Chilterns, flying its beech-tree standards, juts boldly out to meet the sweep of Quarry Woods on the Berkshire bank, and, beneath the heights of Wittington and Danesfield, falls to the river at Hurley in the only sheer cliff the Thames encounters in all its varied course. The pleasant town of Marlow, sheltering beneath it, has many memories. Here came Shelley in 1817 with Mary Godwin, whom he had lately made his legal wife. His friend, Peacock, author of *Headlong Hall* and *Crotchet Castle*, was already living there, and secured for him Albion House in West Street. Shelley signed a twenty-one years' lease, and contrived to stay there eleven months—possibly the most peaceful period in all his restless life. He wrote diligently, completing works so varied as *The Revolt of Islam* and *Proposals for putting Reforms to the Vote, by the Hermit of Marlow,* and Mary Shelley finished *Frankenstein.* Leigh Hunt came down to see them and to borrow money; Mary's father paid long visits, expounding his Utopian dreams; Thomas Hogg, Shelley's college friend and future biographer, was a frequent guest. Together these bright spirits explored and enjoyed the district. " We took many walks in all directions from Marlow," wrote Peacock at a later date, " saw everything worth seeing at a distance of sixteen miles. This comprehended, among other notable places, Windsor Castle and Forest, Virginia Water, and the spots which were consecrated by the memories of Cromwell, Hampden and Milton, in the Chiltern district of Buckinghamshire. . . ." At times the stalwart fellows tramped on foot all the way from London.

A resident in Marlow at that time gives a vivid picture of the poet in a letter to Lady Shelley, quoted in Professor Dowden's *Life*. " I have often met him going or coming from his island retreat near Medmenham Abbey. He was the most interesting figure I ever saw; his eyes like a deer's, bright but rather wild; his white throat unfettered; his slender, but to me almost faultless shape . . . are as fresh in my recollection as an occurrence of yesterday. . . . Sometimes he was rather fantastically arrayed: on his head would be a wreath of what in Marlow we call ' old man's beard ' and wild flowers intermixed. . . ." He did much of his writing on one or other of the islands beneath the many weirs at Hurley,

> " where with sound like many voices sweet,
> Waterfalls leap among wild islands green
> Which framed for my lone boat a lone retreat."

The village of Medmenham lies in a hollow beyond the promontory. Its interesting past has been recorded by its vicar, the Rev. A. H. Plaisted, in what is surely one of the best parish histories ever published. Close by the river lies the Abbey, where the eccentric Sir Francis Dashwood of West Wycombe founded the first of country clubs on the old monastic foundations. His political enemies connected its name with " Hell-fire," but there is much to be said for a country club which admitted only wits and men of taste and scholarship as members; nor is there any real evidence that Dashwood and his boon companions behaved worse here than elsewhere. The Abbey has had further vicissitudes since then, and is now a very well-kept private residence. A lane runs past it from the ferry to the cross-roads with many pleasant pictures by the way. Yew Tree Cottage, a fifteenth-century building, now divided into three, stands near the ancient church; and equally attractive is

ABOVE MEDMENHAM.

the group formed at a corner of the main road by the old chalk post office, smothered in creepers, with its attendant cottages, backed by the great chalk quarry that gave them birth. Above the village the ground rises steeply; on the left a bare patch of open down is crowned by the Jacobean gables of Lodge Farm, whence Mr. Bathurst has made his drawing of the hills and valley towards Fawley, and on the right a covering of beeches conceals the mounds and trenches that were once the Norman castle of the Bolebecs. The gorge between them is no bad starting-place for walks. We can wander up through rolling country to Bockmer on the hilltop, dive down into the secluded valley of Finnamore Farm—a perfect homestead in a perfect setting—and finally descend by Booker Common and its adjoining woods to the Wycombe valley; or, turning to the right at the Stokenchurch road and passing the end of the lane that leads to the interesting old home of the Knights Hospitallers at Widmer, follow the long hill down to Marlow with glorious views of the river valley and ridge upon ridge of the Windsor Forest country opening before us all the way.

But we are bound for Oxfordshire, and must push forward up the river. The narrow strip of level ground that lies between the Chilterns and the Thames from Hambleden to Henley saw much guerrilla fighting in the Civil War. Fawley Court, best known to rowing men as the half-way house on the famous Regatta course, was the home of the eminent Roundhead Bulstrode Whitelocke, who sat for Great Marlow in the Long Parliament; Greenlands, just below the starting-point, belonged to the Royalist D'Oyleys; and here, alongside the later battle-fields of the oarsmen of Thames and London, of New College and Trinity Hall, of Pennsylvania and Leander, the two houses carried on a little warfare of their own and both were reduced to ruins. Fawley Court was soon rebuilt from designs by Sir Christopher Wren, with decorations by Grinling Gibbons, and more than once was honoured by royal visits in the days of the Georges and William IV. But Greenlands house and grounds only attained their present form in our own day from the hands of Mr. W. H. Smith and his son, Lord Hambleden. Where the Fawley property meets the deer-park of Henley Park we cross the Oxfordshire boundary and are soon in Henley.

A single week in the year brings sufficient fame to Henley to render description needless. The old church tower, with its chequered pattern of black flint and white stone, and the graceful arches of the bridge, are familiar to many who know little more of the river or the hills that give to Henley reach its peculiar beauty than can be seen from the regatta course. Numbers of those who have passed beneath the bridge have failed to observe the sculptured heads that decorate the top of the centre arch on either side—old Thames is looking down the stream and the youthful Isis looking up. Yet, as Horace Walpole remarked, " The keystones of a county bridge designed and carved by a young lady is an unparalleled curiosity! " They were the work of the sculptress Mrs. Anne Damer, daughter of General Conway, Walpole's friend and cousin, who lived at Park Place on the hill above; and the head of Isis is said to be a portrait of her friend Miss Freeman of Fawley Court. Yet if we resolutely turn our backs on the river, Henley has still many attractions for us: it is an admirable centre for exploring the tangle of woods and valleys and curly lanes with sweeping downs beyond, which covers the 66,000 acres of the Oxfordshire Chilterns.

Above Henley the Thames valley turns sharply south, to Reading, and then curves back more gradually to the north till it frees itself from the guidance of the hills beyond Goring. This great loop is completely filled by the tail end of the Chiltern range. From Henley Reading is but eight miles distant and Goring twelve, and the high road running north-west to Oxford crosses the whole ridge from Bix Hill to Gangsdown Hill at Huntercombe in little more than five miles; so that the whole of this Chiltern buttress is easily accessible to the walker from Henley. The towns and villages of the river-side need not detain us. Beauties they have in plenty of their own type. The Thames is at its best; the rose-gardens on its banks are famous, and many of the newer houses peep pleasantly from among the trees. But with all its charm of water, woods and hills, the valley lacks the genuine Chiltern flavour. Many a good walk on the hilltops may have a happy ending in delightful river prospects as we descend to Pangbourne or to Goring, but we are conscious all the time that we are treading different ground and have left behind us the seclusion and the subtlety which mark the Penn Country. Here and there riparian towns are pushing outliers up the slope, but always, before they attain the summit ridges, great woodlands, planted by nature or by man, stretch out to meet and to engulf them. The advance from Shiplake has quickened its pace in the last few years, but across its path stands Crowsley Park, the ancient home of the Baskervilles. Its seven great avenues have been famous for centuries, and their beauties are challenged to-day by its gardens, where formal walks of classic stateliness end in a rampant wilderness of blossoming shrubs and hardy flowers. Hidden by its trees, the wave of villas and bungalows is creeping near on the Henley side, but we rely on Crowsley Park to be our Verdun—" *ils ne passeront pas.*" For surely no vandal could have the heart to mar its beauties. The firs and beeches on the hills of Wyfold Court carry on the line in face of the Caversham salient, and then the wide expanse of College Wood bestrides the ridge, till we can look down into the vale on the further side. The heights behind these barriers still retain their full Chilternity. An occasional blot may be found, usually due to the uninstructed fancy of a local builder: here and there " government surplus " huts or corrugated iron roofs intrude to give the rising generation a taste of the horrors of war. But these occur but seldom, and are easily overlooked among the trees. The massed attacks of the dashing bungaliers are well behind us, and for the most part we can follow lane or footpath this way or that as the fancy leads us, and never go far wrong.

The readiest way to reach the summit from Henley is to take the Oxford road as far as Nettlebed, nor, for once, need the walker shrink from a main highway. From the end of busy Bell Street we pass almost at once into open country and, following the valley to the left, enter the stretch of road known as the Fair Mile. It runs dead straight up the bottom for nearer two miles than one, but the folds of the hills on either side give variety to the views, and we walk all the way through an avenue, which has hitherto escaped the baneful eye of the Road Board. These elms were planted in the first half of the eighteenth century by Sir William Stapleton of Greys Court, over the hill on our left, which we shall visit later; long may his good deed live after him! At the end of the Fair Mile our road curves to the left up Bix Hill, while a winding lane follows the narrowing bottom forward to Stonor and to Pishill and to many another delectable hamlet even smaller and more remote. We find Bix Hill a sufficiently arduous climb, and it must have been a far more difficult obstacle before the skill of Telford and Macadam put surfaces on English roads. One can feel for the Henley carriers who protested to King James I against the law which forbade them to yoke more than five horses in a cart. But backward views of the valley which we have left, with the broken outline of Henley Park behind it, give full excuse for halts before we reach the summit. Passing through the village of Bix we plunge into deep woodlands from which we emerge to find ourselves on Nettlebed Common, and so come abruptly into the narrow, old-fashioned street of Nettlebed itself.

Along this road, disguised as the groom of Mr. John Ashburnham, rode King Charles I in the spring of 1646, having successfully evaded the Parliamentary forces closing in on Oxford and started on the long journey which was to end a month later in his unwise surrender to the Scottish army at Newark; and along the same way in 1782, when Stapleton's trees were still young, came a more appreciative traveller from Germany, whose experiences (translated into English) we may read in the chronicles of " British Tourists " collected by the discerning Dr. Mavor. Karl Philipp Moritz was at this time a young schoolmaster at Dessau; but during a visit to Rome four years later he met Goethe, who at once recognized his abilities, and shortly afterwards he was appointed Professor of Archæology and Æsthetics at Berlin. His *Reisen eines Deutschen in England* was published in 1788 after his two novels had made his reputation as a writer. During his short visit to England he studied many sides of London with an observant eye, and then set off to walk by Oxford to Derbyshire, where the caverns of the Peak and the underground streams were beginning to attract the attention of scientists. Setting off from Richmond with a knapsack on his back, he delighted in the green hedges by the road and the variety of scene that makes England a paradise for walkers. In his pocket he carried a copy of his favourite English poet, " and when I was tired," he says, " I sat down in the shade under one of these hedges and read Milton." His only difficulty was in obtaining decent lodging for the night. To-day, to walk is something of a distinction, but in the days of George III all people of consequence, when they travelled, either rode a horse or drove in chaise or coach. " A traveller on foot in this country," he complains, " seems to be considered as a sort of wild man or an out of the way being, who is stared at, pitied, and shunned by everybody that meets him." He was refused a bed at Eton, and was scurvily treated in the inn at Windsor. At the end of a good day's tramp he arrived at Henley, to-day so hospitable to strangers; but at every inn at which he knocked the answer was the same—" We have got no beds, you can't stay here to-night! "

" It was the same," he continues, " at another house on the road. I was therefore obliged to determine to walk on as far as Nettlebed, which was five miles farther, where I arrived rather late in the evening.

" Everything seemed to be alive in this little village; there was a party of militia, who were dancing, singing and making merry. Immediately on my very entrance into the village, the first house, lying on my left, was an inn, from which, as is usual in England, a large beam extended across the Street to the opposite house from which hung dangling an astonishing large sign with the name of the proprietor.

12

" ' May I stop here to-night? ' I asked with eagerness. ' Why yes, you may. . . .'

" When I retired I was shown into a carpeted bed-room, with a very good bed; and next morning I put on clean linen and dressed myself as well as I could. . . . It being Sunday, all the family were in their best attire. I now began to be much pleased with this village, and so I resolved to stop at it and attend divine service. The prayer book which my landlord lent me was quite a family piece: for all his children's births and names, and also his own wedding-day, were very carefully set down in it. Even on this account alone the book would not have been uninteresting to me.

" At half-past nine the service began. Directly opposite to the inn, the boys of the village were all drawn up, as if they had been recruits to be drilled: all well-looking healthy lads, neat and decently dressed, and with their hair cut short, according to the English fashion. Their bosoms were open, and the white frills of their shirts turned back on each side. They seemed to be drawn up here, at the entrance to the village, merely to wait the arrival of the clergyman. At length came the parson on horseback. The boys pulled off their hats and all made him very low bows. He appeared to be rather an elderly man, and wore his own hair, round and decently dressed; or rather curling naturally.

" The bell now rung in, and so I too, with a sort of secret proud sensation, as if I also had been an English-man, went with my prayer-book under my arm to church, along with the rest of the congregation. . . ."

With everything he saw, the spell of Nettlebed grew stronger, and after the service he still lingered in the place.

" I seemed indeed to be enchanted, as if I could not leave this village. Three times did I get off, in order to go on further, and as often returned, more than half resolved to spend a week or more in my favourite Nettle-bed. But the recollection that I had but a few weeks to stay in England, and that I must see Derbyshire, at length drove me away. I cast back many a longing, lingering look on the little Church Steeple, and those hospitable friendly roofs where, all that morning I had found myself so perfectly at home. . . .

" The road from Nettlebed seemed to me but as one long fine gravel walk in a neat garden. And my pace in it was varied, like that of one walking in a garden—I sometimes walked quick, then slow; and then sat down and read Milton. . . ."

Nettlebed has naturally seen some changes in a century and a half, but they are not obtrusive. The old house at the left-hand corner is no longer an inn, with sign slung high athwart the street, but its roof is surely that which sheltered Moritz. The church at the further end has been rebuilt, but does not look aggressively new. One still gets the same feeling of exhilaration when one emerges from the shade of the surrounding forests and suddenly finds oneself in the sunshine of the common. Nettlebed gives a sense of height far beyond the 700 feet or so which unimaginative surveyors grant it. There is a spaciousness about it that makes the woods below seem stuffy, and the air blows fresh and clean from any point of the compass. One has so obviously reached the top that one has no need to be told that Nettlebed Common contains the ultimate summit of the Chiltern range before it descends to the Thames. Apart from its situation, the village has a decided charm of its own. The main street follows the Oxford road, which curves to give a certain unexpectedness to the views at either exit; it contains many old houses of character, and the inns that stand at either side, the " White Hart " and the " Bull," recall the coaching days. But all around the common roads and tracks lead us to isolated groups of cottages or houses in little gardens, hidden by gorse and bracken from the main road, which account for half the village population.

It is to be regretted that the church, which was rebuilt in 1846, contains so little of the earlier edifice. The finely painted Royal Arms of George II, which were then discarded, to-day adorn the clubroom of the " Bull." But the old church had received much rough handling and was possibly beyond repair. In the Civil War it was occupied for some years by Parliamentary soldiers, who were accustomed to light their fires on one of the Taverner tombs, till the inscription was obliterated and eventually the stone split in pieces; and, long before this, like other churches, it had been robbed of many of its ornaments and endowments by the King's Commissioners at the time of the Reformation. It is pleasant to know that a Nettle-bed woman saved from the wreck the bequest she had made towards the lighting of the building. The church-wardens were obliged to report that

" One Anne Eaton, wydowe, gent. dyd gyve towards the mayntenance of a lampelight in the same parishe churche one cowe price 10s., whiche cowe the said Anne Eaton dyd withdrawe when all the lyghts in the churche was put downe, and the said Anne Eaton ys now deceased."

Anthony à Wood, the seventeenth-century author of *Athenæ Oxonienses* quotes in his parochial collections many inscriptions from the old church. His friend Dr. John Wallis, who, as keeper of the University records, had rendered him great assistance in his researches into Oxford history, married a Taverner of Soundess Court in this parish, a property which eventually passed to the Wallis family through the extinction of the senior lines. Some of these Taverner monuments have been replaced in the south aisle of the present building, and the perfection of their lettering and spacing, which seems to have been a natural gift to craftsmen of that day, puts many a modern inscription to shame. The earliest Taverner whose memory is here perpetuated is Edmund, younger son of Richard Taverner, " Clerke of ye Signett to K. Hen: ye 8th & High Sherife of this county." A younger Edmund, grandson of Richard, also found employment under the King, and " after twelve yeeres paynfull service in Courtt, dying there, rests here from his labours." His virtues are celebrated in a six-line poem. The last of the name was John Taverner, some time high sheriff

of Oxfordshire, who was born in the reign of Queen
Elizabeth, lived through the Civil War, and died in 1674,
having outlived his three sons. Soundess Court, which
lies about half a mile north of the village, has been restored and refronted to such an extent that from the gate
it looks like a modern building. But the best testimony to
its old importance is to be found in Nettlebed Common.
The main roads and the lanes leading to scattered groups
of houses run across it open to the sky, through low-
growing gorse and bracken. High trees appear only on
its outer fringes except at one place, where a lane leading
out of the common is deeply shadowed by a thick avenue.
This leads straight to Soundess Court. There are no
houses beyond it; the lane runs direct and purposeful as
far as its gate, and then meanders pleasantly down into
a narrow glen between high walls of larches and so curls
gradually downwards to join the Stonor Valley. The
avenue obviously points to the home of the Taverners
and nowhere else. With this house, as with so many other
houses in the district, the name of Nell Gwynn has been
connected, and the Ordnance Map boldly attaches to it
the secondary title of " Nell Gwynn's Bower " in all the
glory of mediæval type. But it is hard to find any substantial evidence in support of the story. One doubts
if " pretty witty Nelly " from Drury Lane would have
appreciated its solitude and the natural beauty of its surroundings. Still more difficult is it to believe the local
legend that she threw her jewels into its well, where they
still remain. Her nearest proven home was Burford
House in Windsor, granted to her for life by King Charles
II, who was never accustomed to hide his mistresses in
secret bowers. Oral traditions aver that she paid calls
at various Chiltern houses in company with her royal
lover. She may have come to Nettlebed; she may have
admired some bower; but, that she ever lived at Soundess
sufficiently long to construct one and see the roses and the
honeysuckle grow about it, is very doubtful.

To the west of the avenue, close to the Stokenchurch
road, the common rises to a knoll, only slightly higher than
the rest but high enough to give it the greatest elevation in

the neighbourhood. On its summit is the artificial mound upon which stood the famous windmill of Nettlebed. Alas, that one should have to use the past tense! It was burnt down in 1912. It was a very good windmill in itself, and was so placed as to take exactly the right position in a picture, whether seen from the common or rising above the village street. It gave the rounded hill an apex, and was a landmark to the weary traveller from the moment he broke from the woods or topped the ridge at any point from Stoke Row to Beacon Hill. Tradition says that it was first erected at Watlington down in the valley, but lack of wind caused its removal, in its entirety, to this hill top, drawn by sixteen horses on two timber carts. I can vouch for the fact that the view from the upper windows was glorious. On any ordinary day Windsor Castle looked very near with forest ridges stretching far beyond it. The whole line of the Cotswolds was prominent, and through gaps in the North Downs only the intervention of the South Downs prevented a clear view to the sea. North and east, when the shadows fell obliquely, one could distinguish the complicated succession of spurs and valleys in the Chiltern system. It was never my luck to come to the windmill at one of those moments of perfect clearness when observers could note the glint of the sun on the glass roof of the Crystal Palace, or see the Isle of Wight breaking away from the Hampshire coast. Given the day and the hour, the eye can achieve distances that seem incredible. I have sat on little Mount Belinda, where France meets Italy, and seen the snow mountains of Corsica rise from the Mediterranean; from Great Gable I have traced the whole coast line of Lancashire, with the mountains of North Wales projecting to the west; and on a memorable day, when I tramped through Thomas Ingoldsby's country from Canterbury to Hythe, I saw an unbelievable stretch of France from the downs above Folkestone race-course, looking right through to the green hills that lie behind the salient of Ypres. At such a moment I can well believe anything told of Nettlebed.

The view only fell short of perfection because it lacked

a middle distance. The mill sat on its rounded summit like the button on a mandarin's hat, and the brim of the hill above the escarpment cut off everything between the foreground of woods and commons and the downs far across the Thames. But this only serves to give us a new prospect when we have covered the mile and three-quarters to the edge of Nuffield Common, where the golfers of Huntercombe enjoy their game amid glorious surroundings. Here we look straight down upon the plain, with Wittenham Clumps standing out across the Thames as the most prominent feature. It is a fine view of rural England as it was. No big town intrudes upon the landscape; the double names of the villages recall old times and ancient manors—Crowmarsh Gifford and Berrick Salome, Brightwell Baldwin and Clifton Hampden, Drayton St. Leonard's and Nuneham Courtenay—and most of them are worth a close inspection by any lover of antiquity. Past the projecting nose of Swyncombe Down we look over Chalgrove Field to the ridge above the Thame that bears the precious burden of Garsington and Cuddesdon.

We will return to Henley by Stoke Row which lies all along the ridge which forms the next downward step towards the Thames. We cross Nuffield Common to the left, past the little church in its grove of fir trees. The road we follow to Ipsden Heath gives views alternately on either side before plunging into woodlands. Here—two miles from Nuffield—diverging roads invite us in many directions. By bearing to the right we can descend to Ipsden by Berin's Hill, where St. Birinus preached, and find, in the thicket to the right, a little well said to be Roman. It gained a certain notoriety some years ago when a vagrant threw into it her unwanted child: the child was caught in overhanging boughs and rescued unharmed. If we follow the escarpment forward, we can come to Checkendon and reach the Thames at Goring. But for Henley we bear to the left and enter the long straight road that runs through the straggling village of Stoke Row.

Stoke Row has had a long and honourable connexion

with the family of Reade of Ipsden. There are memorials to fifteenth-century " Redes " in the little Norman church at Checkendon, and a member of the family defended his house near Abingdon against the Roundheads until it was burnt about him. Its best-known son was the novelist Charles Reade, who introduces the village as " Hillstoke " in his novel, *A Woman-hater*. Uxmore Farm, which we pass on the left, gave a title to his whiskered hero " Lord Uxmoor," and his pictures of the place were drawn from his early memories, when the road still ran across an open common. Behind the new fences, which now enclose it, we can see the old hedges with a generous stretch of grass between.

" The cottages," he writes, " were white as snow and thatched as at Islip; but instead of vegetable gardens they all had orchards. The trees were apple and cherry: of the latter not less than a thousand in that small hamlet. It was literally a lawn, a quarter of a mile long and about two hundred yards broad, bordered with white cottages and orchards. The cherries, red and black, gleamed like countless eyes among the cool leaves. There was a little church on the lawn that looked like a pigeon-house. A cow or two grazed peacefully. . . . The village and its turf lay in the semicircular sweep of an unbroken forest; but at the sides of the leafy basin glades had been cut for drawing timber, stacking bark, etc.; and what Milton calls so happily ' the chequered shade ' was seen in all its beauty; for the hot sun struggled in at every aperture, and splashed the leaves and the path with fiery flashes and streaks, and topaz brooches, all intensified in fire and beauty by the cool adjacent shadows."

The further end of the village, where the common still lies open, is at all times beautiful; the earlier portion of the road, straitly confined and bordered by several new houses of incongruous design, may often disappoint searchers for the village of Reade's description. But the cherry trees are still there, and when they come out in flower, with each white blossom showing up against the woods behind, the whole place is transformed into a fairy-land that no new blots can spoil. There are many glorious

THE MAHARAJAH'S WELL: STOKE ROW.

cherry orchards in the Penn Country, but nowhere do they seem so entirely to influence the scene.

One of the many plots of Reade's story hangs on the inadequacy of the Hillstoke water supply: the village drew its water, like many another, from the stagnant ponds. In these waterless tracts one can well understand the benefit great lords bestowed upon their free and customary tenants by sinking wells such as we see at Turville Heath or Grey's Court; and we can sympathize with the veneration paid to the wells themselves which made the Creator's gift available to men. Centuries after St. Birinus preached on Berin's Hill, St. Hugh of Avalon, Bishop of Lincoln, had occasion to reprove the people of High Wycombe for well-worship, as a practice lending itself to superstitious uses; but here, above the water line, his inhibition can have carried little weight, and the scarcity of wells long continued. A dry summer is still recalled in Stokenchurch when beer was cheaper than water; and even in the last few years water has been carted to certain Chiltern villages and retailed at half-a-crown a barrel or twopence for the smallest quantity. The crying need of Stoke Row was answered in a curious way. At the end of a short avenue of cypresses, that runs from the road in the middle of the village, stands a magnificent well, with the figure of an elephant above the shaft, surmounted by an Oriental cupola. Round the top runs the legend, " His Highness the Maharajah of Benares, India, gave this Well, 1864." Its perfect symmetry can be seen in Mr. Bathurst's drawing, but what does it here? Charles Reade was the youngest of seven sons, and five of his elder brothers entered the East India Company's Service. The fifth, Sir Edward Reade, became Commissioner of Benares in 1846 and won the lasting gratitude of the inhabitants by his work on behalf of the College, the blind asylum, and the dispensaries. During the Mutiny, on the death of the military commander, he successfully conducted the defence of Agra, and when he retired in 1860 he received grateful addresses from the loyal Indians of Agra and Benares. In India he had spoken of the waterless character of his native district, and the Maharajah of Benares, knowing the horrors of drought and wishing to give him some token of his esteem, decided to erect this well, 368 feet deep, in the corner of the Reade estate. A Reade still takes his place among the guardian trustees.

At the end of the village, the road descends a hill through woods and rises again to climb the beautiful slope of common and orchard crowned by Witheridge Hill. Near this delightful little hamlet four ancient parishes used to meet. Mongewell and Newnham Murren ran side-by-side in long narrow strips to the Thames near Wallingford, while Rotherfield Grays and Rotherfield Peppard similarly extended to the river south of Henley; all were largely composed of high pastures and woodland, and guarded their corridors to the water as jealously as any Baltic State. From the dip beyond Witheridge Hill we can shorten our walk by taking a footpath that rejoins the road near Shepherd's Green; we have fine views down the Peppard hollow, and backward on our right to Wyfold Court rising well among the trees. This is a fine modern hall, but it stands on an earlier site and the property is held by a curious tenure: the owner must be prepared to present his sovereign with a rose if he or she should chance to pass on a May Day.

Where the War Memorial Cross divides the road at the end of Grey's Green, the right arm leads to Rotherfield Greys church and village, the left to Grey's Court. We will first look into the church and then take the short cross-road to the Court. The church was probably Norman before it was rebuilt in 1200, in Early English style with an apse, by Walter de Grey, Archbishop of York and Chancellor of the Kingdom in the reign of John. There is a fine brass on the floor of the chancel to Robert de Grey (1387) last Lord Grey of Grey's Court, fully accoutred with hauberk and bassinet, baldric and rowelled spurs: but the chapel constructed by the Knollys family, who owned Grey's Court in the days of the Tudors, holds a far more elaborate monument. This is the altar tomb of Sir Francis Knollys, Treasurer to Queen Elizabeth, and his wife, erected in 1605 by their son William Knollys, Earl of Banbury. They lie side-by-side, in coloured alabaster, on the raised tomb, with their seven sons and seven daughters kneeling on the floor around them: a chrysom child—one who died before baptism—lies, like a doll, on the slab beside the mother, and, on the top of the tester above, the Earl and Countess of Banbury kneel at a prayer-desk. The workmanship is wonderful, but it is difficult to get a complete view of the tomb in this cramped space. The organ has been placed under the arch leading to the chapel and prevents any sight of the whole monument from the nave. The church would gain enormously by its removal.

Grey's Court, which lies across a little valley from the church, has by far the most romantic appearance of any building in the district. The three great towers of the original fortress, with a good length of curtain wall about them, rising on a hill in the deer park, catch the eye to the exclusion of the later residence, which was built by the Knollys family within the old fortifications in the more pacific days of the Tudors. The towers suggest a north-country stronghold like Richmond or Barnard Castle, rather than anything near the Thames Valley, and their first owners, the Greys, had a strong connexion with the North Riding. Walter de Grey, who built it, was Archbishop of York, and John, the second baron of Rotherfield, who had licence to crenellate it in 1348, fought gallantly against the Scots and married two Yorkshire heiresses. Sir Walter Scott would have loved it for itself, and none the less because its owner brought Avice de Marmion to be its mistress. It was probably damaged after the rebellion of Lord Lovell, to whom it passed by marriage, and was a ruin when Leland came to view it in the following reign. " There appere," he writes, " entering into the maner place on the righte hand three or four very olde towers of stone, a manifest to men it was some tyme a castle." The old well-house still contains, in good condition, the great wheel 75 feet in circumference within which the donkey used to walk to draw the water. The present mansion, which, with its outbuildings, embodies walls of the original fortress, still retains Elizabethan and Jacobean features. It passed in the later seven-

teenth century to another Yorkshire family, the Staple-
tons, who still possess it.

We are now within two miles of Henley. We follow
the sloping ridge that lies between the Fair Mile and the
Peppard hollow, and, passing Badgemore House and Friars
Park, descend the precipitous road that becomes the main
street of the riverside town.

CHAPTER XIV

ON THE ICKNIELD WAY

WE will end, where we began, with the steep escarpment of the Chiltern Hills looking north and west across the Vale. This Chiltern ridge, here forming part of the rim of the great basin in which lies London, is itself a portion of the long line of chalk downland that runs across England, beginning with the Wiltshire Downs and ending in white cliffs above the Wash; and in days long before history its course had been followed by an ancient trackway, connecting the agricultural settlements of East Anglia with the great centres of religion, culture and commerce which to-day only survive in the Standing Stones of Avebury and Stonehenge. If you walk along it—say, from Dunstable to Devizes—you note its convenience for early travellers. All the way from Ivinghoe Beacon till you descend amid many barrows from Hackpen Hill to Avebury, the edge of the hill is an unmistakable guide, for when you come to any gap the next length of grassy wall is always clearly visible beyond. The hill makes for good going, and on the smooth and open downs of Wiltshire and Berkshire the track runs along the top. But, north of the Thames, different conditions were found by primitive wayfarers. The summits were clothed with impenetrable thickets and the Vale was a swamp in rainy weather: here therefore the old road runs along the chalk close below the ridge. This length is more particularly called the Icknield Way to-day, and it serves to tie together the sticks of the open fan that we call the Penn Country.

We have already walked a length of it near Ivinghoe Beacon and can pass quickly over this northern portion, where it is now overlaid by a modern road of some importance. Its course has been diverted in places; near Ivinghoe we can see the old track curling away beside the new, where the route was straightened a century ago. But, for the most part it is difficult to picture the old British track beneath the tarmac surface. The road is a constant switchback, rising where the foothills thrust out spurs into the Vale, and descending again to the lowest level that gives a solid chalk foundation. These constant ascents, and particularly the long climb up the Aston Clinton hill, constrained early travellers to take to the Vale when the ground was dry and firm, and so mark out the course of the Lower Icknield Way. But such opportunities were infrequent: the Romans made a bend in Akeman Street in order to have the assistance of the long Aston spur in crossing the valley, and even when Leland passed in Tudor days a raised causeway was still required from Wendover to Aylesbury, " els the way in wett tyme as in a low stiff claye were taedious and ill to passe." The upper track has always been the Icknield Way *par excellence,* and the fact that its course is laid just where the chalk first appears has made it a curious geological boundary. This was noted more than a century ago by St. John Priest, when he came to study the county as one of King George III's agricultural commissioners.

" Upon the side of these hills in some parts, and at their foot in others, lies the Ikenild Way, which runs through the county; and which would not be noticed in this place, did not a remarkable circumstance attend it in its progress, perhaps accidentally, which is, that on the right hand side of it, towards the valley, the soil is so good a mixture of clay and chalk, as to be worth for a furlong in breadth, according to the estimate of farmers situated near it, at least 10s. an acre to hire, more than that on the left hand, between it and the hills. This circumstance was observed by Sir John Dashwood King, Bart., and his tenants at Halton, as well as by Mr. Grace at Risborough. It is not wonderful that the lowest lands should be made richer than lands lying by the side of hills; but it is remarkable that this Roman road should thus separate for a considerable way lands so distinct from each other in quality."

The Wendover gap is easily crossed on comparatively high ground, and thenceforward the Icknield Way has greater attractions for the walker. We have not yet reached the primitive British track we shall find further on, but it is a country lane instead of a high road that we follow. There is less traffic, and the ups and downs, shorter and more frequent, give greater variety to the views. We follow the straight line of the ridge crowned by the Ellesborough monument, and from the top of the spur beneath it look up a peaceful little valley to the woods of Chequers and across it to the church of Ellesborough— a notable landmark superbly planted on its own little mound projecting into the Vale. This is the parish church of Chequers, and several members of the Russell family, who lived there in the eighteenth-century, are buried in the churchyard. Within the church there is a fine marble monument bearing an effigy of Brigitta Lady Croke, the heiress of the Hawtreys, who died in 1638. From here to Great Kimble the road is bordered on the left by the demesne of Chequers. At first the ground slopes gently backward to the hill, but near the Kimbles a great headland juts out above the road, cleft by a precipitous ravine from the depths of which a clear stream issues. This corner has long been famous for its beauty. The green sward near at hand has been christened the " Velvet Lawn," the source of the brook is " Silver Spring," and round the corner lies the " Happy Valley." A feature of these hills is the number of giant box-trees that grow wild about them. The sceptical gardener, used to box " edgings," must here admit that the bowls men roll on bowling-greens can honestly be carved from box-wood.

In the days of Sir William Hawtrey, who built the manor house in 1566, a very humble and repentant little prisoner was committed to his charge and kept at Chequers for two years " without going abroad." One hopes she was allowed to taste the charming diversity of the park. She was Lady Mary Keys, great-granddaughter of King Henry VII and sister to the still more luckless Lady Jane Grey. Though her claim to the throne was remote, the childless Queen Elizabeth had retained her at court in order that she might keep an eye on her matrimonial projects. Great was the stir when Lady Mary Grey, the tiniest lady in the royal household, was found to have secretly married Thomas Keys, the giant Sergeant Porter, a widower with several children. Keys was sent to the Fleet prison, and his wife to Chequers. Hence she addressed piteous letters to " good Master Secretary " Cecil, " desiringe rather deathe than to be any longer without so greate a well as her majestes favor," and signing them " Mary Graye," as if she could annul her marriage by a stroke of the pen. With the death of her husband her imprisonment became less rigorous. She humbly begged permission to wear mourning: and she was still humble when she made her own will seven years later:

" As for my body, I commit the same to be buried where the Queen's majesty shall think most meet and convenient. . . . To my very good lady and grandmother, the Duchess of Suffolk her grace, one pair of bracelets of gold with a jank-stone in each bracelet, or else my jewel of unicorn's horn, whichsoever liketh her grace best to take . . ."

At the corner of the park of Chequers we pass the diminutive church of Little Kimble and are soon descending to the cross-roads at Great Kimble. These villages are said to derive their name from the British king Cunobelinus, father of Caractacus, whose legendary history forms the basis of Shakespeare's *Cymbeline*; and the name of Cymbeline's Mount has been attached to the spur covered by earthworks near Chequers. Since this prince died before the first organized Roman invasion in the reign of the Emperor Claudius, the lack of historical support is hardly surprising. Nor is it wise to dismiss entirely local tradition. Country memories are long. A mound rising above Princes Risborough, which we are approaching, has been called Soldiers Hill from time immemorial, nobody having the slightest idea who the soldiers were. Excavations undertaken in modern times have led to the discovery of coins of Constantine the Great, and it is not beyond the bounds of possibility that the name has been handed down from one rustic mouth to another since the Roman eagles were raised upon its summit.

"It is said" must again be written against the story that it was at Great Kimble Church that John Hampden made his first protest against the payment of ship-money. Carlyle's stirring and circumstantial account of the scene, as vivid as if he had stood among the crowd and watched it, would win over many a jury; but here the paucity of contemporary evidence is more damaging. The church has been radically restored since Hampden's day.

The main road continues its descent till we stand almost on the floor of the Vale near Monks Risborough. But the old Icknield Way will have none of this, and, bending away to the left, follows the roots of the hills. It ascends to a considerable height in the hamlet of Whiteleaf, and, passing close beneath the great white cross on the hillside, makes a long semicircular detour up the ensuing valley in order to cross the pass near the watershed and so gain the firm ground on the slopes of Bledlow Ridge. For, apart from the passage of the river Thames, the Risborough gap must have been far the most formidable obstacle to be surmounted by prehistoric travellers between Dunstable and Avebury. Deep drainage was still in its infancy when Burke farmed at Butlers Court. In the Middle Ages narrow causeways were built up to carry a road across wet lands like these, but, even when St. John Priest came this way in the last years of the eighteenth century, the way was bordered by swamp. "In riding from Risborough to Bledlow," he writes, "I turned my chaise out of the road to avoid a waggon, and my horse fell into a bog up to his chest." Only in very recent years has Princes Risborough enjoyed a direct road across the low ground lying between the town and the railway station.

13

The two Risboroughs, like Kings and Abbots Langley, give in their names a clue to their feudal history. Monks Risborough was granted to the monks of Christ Church, Canterbury, long before the Conquest, and remained in their hands until the Dissolution. In the time of Edward the Confessor Princes Risborough was held by Earl Harold, who succeeded him on the throne of England, and it remained a royal appanage for centuries. Henry III gave it to his brother, Prince Richard, Earl of Cornwall and King of the Romans, and from him it passed in turn to his son, Earl Edmund, the founder of the College at Ashridge. Thus Edward the Black Prince, whose name is popularly connected with the place, came late in the list of its princely owners. Both places are interesting, and we shall do well to desert the Icknield way for a time. The old track takes a line from which the new building areas are particularly conspicuous and gives us little of interest in return. We can pass through the Risboroughs and rejoin it above Bledlow without loss.

We come first to Monks Risborough, a peaceful little hamlet with a church sufficiently ancient to have needed a complete restoration in the early fifteenth century. The roof, of that date, is particularly fine, and the rood screen, with the figures of nine of the Apostles rudely painted upon it—the remaining three lost in the course of centuries—is worthy of notice. The church of Princes Risborough, a mile away, has been more drastically restored, but the picturesque little cottage in the corner of the churchyard, which was formerly the Vicarage, has mercifully been left almost untouched, with all the honours of remote antiquity thick upon it. There has been much new building about Princes Risborough since the railway line to London was shortened; but the narrow main street, lined with pleasant old houses, is still a joy to the eye, with the Market House, admirably restored in 1824, completing the picture at the end. In the old days there were great doings here every Christmas. A lady of the Manor, one Joan Chibnall, initiated the custom of giving an early morning feast to the parishioners, which was followed by her successors. Tradition decreed that a fat bull must be killed, a boar be converted into brawn, and four bushels of wheat and four of barley made into bread and beer; and the whole distributed to the inhabitants " in large pieces, smoking hot from the copper," at five o'clock for breakfast on Christmas morning. The popularity of the feast was its undoing. Many of the parishioners paraded the streets all night, causing unseemly disturbance, and there was a general free fight when the victuals were distributed. Eventually a Lord of the Manor took expert advice and found that there was no legal obligation in the matter: and one more good old English custom perished through its abuse.

We cross the railway bridge at Princes Risborough Station and descend to the lowest level of the pass. Here the little village of Saunderton has secured its seclusion by lying a good two miles from its nominal railway station. We are now below the level of the springs, and a fine old moated farm, with real water in its moat and many bulrushes, stands at the corner where we turn to the right for the village of Bledlow. A steady climb lies before us, but we can cut off a corner by taking a footpath to the right near Frogmore Farm. We have now put behind us all the meretricious trappings of modern invasion: henceforth we shall walk as our fathers walked through miles of unspoilt English country. The Icknield Way, running along the hillside not far above us, feels the change, transforming itself back into the same old track of grass and chalk that it was before the first invaders came to Britain: and, down in the valley, the Lower Icknield Way, with its course at times diverted, forms the link between a chain of old-world villages. The two are joined together by many lanes and tracks by which the traveller on the Upper Way can descend to any village that takes his fancy. Between the two lies Bledlow, the first-fruits of our new emancipation. It stands high upon the foothills with its houses scattered down the slope, a place of old brick walls and gables, with here and there a roof of thatch; clipped yews of intricate design before the better houses and a blaze of flowers in cottage gardens. It is bisected by a deep ravine, not unlike the Silver Spring

13*

at Chequers, in the bottom of which many springs gush
out to form the tiny river Glyde. Clumps of massive
wych-elms hang on to its banks by their eyelids, the pools
below are green with watercress, and a pleasant path runs
along the top. Right on the edge stands the ancient flint-
built church, a position which called forth an early
prophecy:

> " They who live and do abide
> Shall see Bledlow Church fall into the Glyde ;
> And they who live and do remain
> Shall see the church built up again."

The road that runs past Bledlow Church and just above
the brink of its neighbouring chasm turns sharply to the
right a few yards further on and descends the hill. Here
a footpath strikes half right, leading down to the lower
road not far from Chinnor, and a track runs up through
the Warren to join the Icknield Way as it coasts round
Wain Hill. If you wish to see as picturesque a line of
unspoilt villages as you could find if you searched all
England, take the lower way. Wander round the square
of old-world streets in Chinnor; note the hall at the end
of Crowell, with its curious windows and many corners,
where old Squire Ellwood bullied his Quaker son; and at
Lewknor seek out the quaint little church and descend the
lane to see the Manor House and the moated grange of
Moor Court. So you will come by Aston Rowant and
Shirburne Castle to the market town of Watlington and
marvel at the cunning brickwork of its old Town Hall.
Thence it is no great distance to the priory of Britwell
Salome and Britwell House, and so over Firebrass Hill to
Ewelme.

But if your fancy leans to wildness and wider views,
come with me to the Icknield Way. Above us rises
Bledlow Ridge, with its Greek cross cut in the turf, a
starting-place for many a notable walk. Below us, on
the right, and all across the Vale little hamlets rise in tufts
amid orchards and lofty elms in a billowy sea of plough-
land. On the left the line of hills becomes more and
more indented and each projecting crest has individual

character. The woods on the top are no longer tidily bobbed and shingled. Some break up into little spinneys; others come straggling all down the side of the hill; patches of gorse and untamed thickets fill the hollows. At times a broken line of stunted firs escorts us on our way. Striking straight from headland to headland the ancient road runs on, regardless of the passing of centuries.

Where the track crosses the road that comes over the hill from Fingest and Turville and descends to Watlington a curious straight line of bared chalk, like the figure 1 written in chalk upon a blackboard, stands out upon the slope. The natives call it the White Mark, but tradition suggests for it no earlier origin than the whim of an eighteenth-century Stonor; its purpose none can guess. A wide coomb lies before us, with Watlington Park crowning the head of the valley and the long ridge of Swyncombe Downs awaiting us on the further side. Dame Alice Farm above us on the left reminds us that we are drawing near our goal: for Dame Alice was Geoffrey Chaucer's granddaughter, and we shall look upon her sad and wistful face, carved in alabaster, when we come to our journey's end at Ewelme. Opposite the tip of Swyncombe Downs an abrupt little hill rises unexpectedly upon the shelving foothills, as if some great lump had rolled down from the top of the escarpment and here come to rest. In a gap between the two high woods upon its summit a great pillar of stone stands out conspicuously. Britwell House itself sits back towards the centre of the hill, an attractive building with lower projecting wings, dating from the reign of Queen Anne. The pillar in front was erected by its builder, Walter Heveringham, in memory of his parents, and is charming in its Addisonian gracefulness and wise economy of ornament. He followed the Old Religion and embodied in his new mansion a shapely chapel with rounded ends and a priest's room adjoining. In the wood at the back is another pillar recalling the earlier history of the site when it held a convent of French nuns. This monument is plain, with no inscription, but it is said to mark the sisters' burial place. The ground about it is thickly carpeted with snowdrops in the early spring, succeeded by the pink-white flowers of a species of fumitory, very rare in England, of which the first roots are thought to have been imported by these pious ladies as a memory of their native France. Doubtful legends of secret underground passages cling to many old houses, but here there is actually one in existence. Walled with brick, it will admit a man stooping; a considerable distance was traversed in a recent exploration before falls of bricks and earth made further progress dangerous, and the tunnel was found to be full of mosquitoes. Its ascertained course forbids the idea that it was anything so prosaic as a drain: for, instead of descending to the lower ground, it starts from the east of the house and curls round the hill to the wood on the west that faces Ewelme. From here the ground falls away on every side, and the strategic importance of the hill to early warriors is obvious. All round its western end it is possible to trace a double line of earthworks. Here the Mercian levies may well have gathered before Offa launched the attack that wrested royal Benson from the kings of Wessex.

At the end of the wood that clothes the foot of Swyncombe Down a narrow lane runs to the left up the precipitous Sliding Hill and over a shoulder to the hollow where Swyncombe House lies beside its Norman church. But we follow the Icknield Way a little further and take the next turning to the right for Ewelme. Cow Common lies open on the left, beyond it is Rabbit Hill, names redolent of rural England; and at the bottom of the gentle valley old cottages and capacious barns peep out beneath great trees. At the first house the road divides, one portion ascending and following the line of the valley just beneath the brow on the right, and the other running down the bottom. Along these two roads and on the steep slope between them lies the peaceful village of Ewelme.

The manor of Swyncombe belonged for centuries to the Abbey of Bec in Normandy, where both Lanfranc and Anselm had already gained a reputation for piety and scholarship before they came to sit in St. Augustine's chair at Canterbury. Confiscated as "enemy property" during the French Wars, it passed to the family of Bacon, who also owned Ewelme, and descended through a chain of heiresses to Matilda Burghersh, who married Thomas Chaucer, son of the poet Geoffrey. Thomas Chaucer was born in 1360 and was a man of importance in his day. He was Steward of the Chiltern Hundreds and Constable of Wallingford Castle, and represented Oxfordshire in parliament for many years; he followed his sovereign to the siege of Harfleur and the field of Agincourt. His only child Alice first married Thomas Montacute, Earl of Salisbury, who was killed at the siege of Orleans, and brought a rich fortune to her second husband, William de la Pole, fourth Earl of Suffolk. Few lives have been so crowded with vicissitudes as that of Alice Chaucer. At first her husband stood high in the councils of the kingdom: he was placed in charge of the boy-king Henry VI and created first Duke of Suffolk for his services. During this period of prosperity, " from love of his wife and the commoditie of her lands," he lived much at Ewelme. But later, in the tangled intrigues of Yorkist and Lancastrian, he came to stand in the path of the future Richard III. The populace turned against him: his life was in danger, and he embarked in a ship for France. His vessel met another in mid-channel, and its skipper met him with the greeting, " Welcome, traitor." He was carried back and murdered in a boat off Dover, his neck being laid upon the gunwale and severed with a rusty sword. His son, John, succeeded to the dukedom as a boy of eight, and his mother had to steer his fortune through stormy seas; but she lived to see him marry Elizabeth Plantagenet, sister of Edward IV and Richard III, and live in almost royal state in the manor house of Ewelme. After their time the glory of the de la Poles died away in a sequence of banishments and attainders. The last of the line fell fighting for the French at the battle of Pavia, and Ewelme soon passed to the Crown.

No English village can boast a finer memorial than that raised by Duke William and Duchess Alice in Ewelme. The old houses of the village lie irregularly all about the place. There is scarcely half a dozen in a row: they sit down where they like on the steep hillside, and a great barn as big as a church intrudes near the end of the only semblance of a street. This not unpleasing disarray gives additional value to the ordered procession of three great buildings, at once dignified and picturesque, all down the hill. Straight from the lower road rises the high brick wall of the School, its windows adorned with heraldic shields and angels carved in stone. Above it, half-way up the slope, and separated from it by an embattled arch-way, stand the almshouses in a peaceful little quadrangle with a well in the middle. A cloister runs all round the inside: carved barge-boards decorate the dormer windows, and tall brick chimneys rise above. From the quadrangle a long flight of steps covered by an arcade ascend steeply to the great west door of the church. In all England it would be difficult to find a group of fifteenth-century buildings so different, so varied, and so little altered.

The church, which lies nearly on a level with the upper road, is a very interesting Perpendicular building. It remains to-day practically as it was rebuilt before the death of Alice Chaucer in 1475. It was miraculously saved from disfigurement both at the time of the Reformation and during the Civil War. Lying in a favourite Royal Manor, it escaped rigorous treatment at the hands of the reformers. A few effigies of saints are missing from their niches, and among the spoils claimed by Edward VI's commissioners were certain vestments worthy of the beautiful church.

" Item: a vestment of whyte and grene damaske with pecockes."
" Item: a vestment of grene damaske with a crosse of roses of gold."

But the fabric remained untouched: and the same good fortune followed it in the Civil War through the championship of Colonel Francis Martyn, an influential officer of Cromwell's army who lived at Ewelme and appreciated its beauties. This gentleman forbade the soldiers to enter

Charles Bathurst 1928

EWELME.

the church except for worship, and a brass in his honour is in the chancel. The church is of an East Anglian type, probably modelled on that of Wingfield, built by the first Earl of Suffolk. At one time it was covered with plaster, but this is now being removed: this operation has unexpectedly revealed the fact that, though the rest of the wall is stone, the battlements are of brick. Mr. Bathurst's drawing shows the church tower rising on the brink of the hill, and its junction with the almshouses below. The whole interior is worthy of study. Just inside the east door is the fifteenth-century font with a tall cover with a figure of St. Michael at the top, elaborately carved. On the corbel behind it is the head of a king with a forked beard identified as Edward III. This king was, according to Speed, " the first raiser of the de la Poles ": in return for a princely subsidy he gave these Hull merchants many manors and showed them great favour. It was probably carved when Duke John married King Edward's descendant, Elizabeth Plantagenet. The north aisle and St. John's Chapel, at its east end, appear to be of slightly later date, possibly added to give seats for the pensioners of the almshouses and the scholars of the school. Between St. John's Chapel and the chancel is the crowning glory of the church, the tomb of the Duchess Alice. It is a masterpiece of alabaster carving. Upon it lies the Duchess, clad in the costume of a vowess with the Garter on her arm. Beneath her is the chest, elaborately carved with shields and figures, containing her remains: and in a chamber below a realistic representation of her skeleton. It is characteristic of early craftsmen, who devoted as much attention to parts not seen as they did to those more prominent, that the ceiling of this lower chamber is adorned with frescoes only visible to one lying on the ground beside it. The richly decorated canopy above is crowned by carved wooden figures. Close by is the altar tomb to the Duchess's parents: the father clad in plate armour with the Chaucer unicorn at his feet, the lady with the forked tailed lion of Burghersh.

In 1437 King Henry VI granted to the first Duke and Duchess of Suffolk a licence " that they, or either the

survivors of them, found an Hospital at the Manor of
Ewelme in the County of Oxford, and settle a sufficient
endowment, not exceeding the yearly value of 200 marks,
for the maintenance of two chaplains and thirteen poor
men to be incorporated and have a common seal." One
of the chaplains was to be Master of the Hospital and the
other teacher of grammar at the school: they were to
receive £10 each a year. The poor men were to have
£3 0s. 8d., one of them, called the Minister, who was set in
authority over the rest, receiving £3 9s. 4d. King James I
gave the Mastership to form an extra endowment for the
Regius Professor of Medicine at Oxford, who still, as
Visitor, holds the post by virtue of his office. The
founders set out their wishes in great detail. The duties
of the Minister, as they were in the early eighteenth
century, are thus quoted by Bishop Rawlinson:

" The account of all the Duty which ought to be done
by the Minister of the Hospital here. In St. John's Chapel
on the South Side of the Church the little Bell is to be
rung at 8 in the morning and at 4 in the afternoon, from
Lady Day to Michaelmas. And from Michaelmas to
Lady Day the same Bell to be rung at 9 in the morning
and 3 in the afternoon. The Minister is to see that the
Pensioners all come to Prayers every day except Holy
Days, Wednesdays and Frydays unless they have leave to
go out or else he is to stop a penny for every day they
miss. The Gutter upon the House next to the Church
is to be weeded and kept clean. Every Pensioner is to
weed his own Plot and keep the Cloysters clean and live
peaceably one with Another. Upon these conditions they
are to be paid every Friday morning upon Chaucer's
Stone 1s 8d. Upon any default they are to be punished
by an abatement of their Salary.
" The Minister is to be a very sober man himself and
keep good hours, he is to have a key of the Church, both
the Cross-doors of the Common Hall, the Treasury, Green
Court Gate, Passage down to the Wood-yard and the
Poor Men's. Every Poor Man is to make use of the
garden Key to go to the Necessary House, or to weed

their gardens, get their wood in, or for any other Convenience.

" The Master and Schoolmaster having a key to all these places to see that every man does his Duty as he ought . . ."

To-day the Minister's office is no longer needed. The Teacher of Grammar has given way to the master of the Elementary School. But the thirteen poor men still enjoy the bounty of Alice Chaucer and her husband, and live in the little quadrangle. Their pay has been increased to 15s. weekly, and coal, doctor and nurse are provided for them. Vacancies are filled by the Lord of the Manor, the Earl of Macclesfield.

The name of Ewelme means the bursting-place of springs: and at the foot of the slope not far below the School one of them gushes out and speeds by the side of the road to join its six sisters in a race to the Thames at Benson. Another rises in the low ground across the road, and the Manor House stands beside it. It is but a shadow of the palace which Duke William and Duchess Alice preferred above their other dwellings—to which Duke John brought his royal bride. Old inventories still recall its ancient glory in their catalogues of great chambers and costly fittings—beds of cloth of gold and satin, a special bed of red sarcenet, broidered with my lord's arms and crest, and all the panoply of the later Middle Ages. The house has had its difficult times, and was once used as a kind of workhouse, sheltering a number of poor families. Since then it has been purchased by the Trustees of Ewelme Hospital, so that Alice Chaucer's birthplace is protected by those who still administer her charity.

The remaining portion of the old palace has been converted into a small, plain and pleasant house, just such a one as you might find in any English hamlet. And it is the same with all the village. It has had its hour of crowded life, and has now returned to be a quiet corner of the English country. Chaucers and De la Poles have passed away: Henry VIII and Catherine Howard might never have crowded its narrow lanes with a train of followers. But through it all, morning after morning, men of Ewelme have driven their cows to Cow Common or pastured their sheep on Rabbit Hill.

Here we end our journey. The Penn Country goes no further. We have beaten its bounds to-day along the Icknield Way. We have seen a fine country, but here and there we have found its repose and beauty threatened by the modern craze for noise and speed—by selfish thoughtlessness or ignorant Vandalism. Here such things fall into their place as a phase that will pass: we have faith that the peace that has returned to Ewelme may still survive throughout the Penn Country.

INDEX

Index

Date Due

		PRINTED IN U. S. A.	